SO YOU WANT TO SING MUSIC THEATER

So You Want to Sing

A Guide for Professionals

A Project of the National Association of Teachers of Singing

So You Want to Sing: A Guide for Professionals is a series of works devoted to providing a complete survey of what it means to sing within a particular genre. Each contribution functions as a touchstone work for not only professional singers, but students and teachers of singing. Titles in the series offer a common set of topics so readers can navigate easily the various genres addressed in each volume. This series is produced under the direction of the National Association of Teachers of Singing, the leading professional organization devoted to the science and art of singing.

So You Want to Sing Music Theater: A Guide for Professionals, by Karen Hall, 2014.

SO YOU WANT TO SING MUSIC THEATER

A Guide for Professionals

Karen Hall

Allen Henderson
Executive Editor, NATS

A Project of the National Association of
Teachers of Singing

ROWMAN & LITTLEFIELD
Lanham • Boulder • New York • Toronto • Plymouth, UK

Published by Rowman & Littlefield
4501 Forbes Boulevard, Suite 200, Lanham, Maryland 20706
www.rowman.com

10 Thornbury Road, Plymouth PL6 7PP, United Kingdom

All photos courtesy of Dr. Scott McCoy.

British Library Cataloguing in Publication Information Available

Library of Congress Cataloging-in-Publication Data

Hall, Karen, 1955– author.
So you want to sing music theater : a guide for professionals / Karen Hall.
pages cm. – (So you want to sing)
Includes bibliographical references and index.
ISBN 978-0-8108-8838-8 (pbk. : alk. paper) – ISBN 978-0-8108-8839-5 (ebook)
1. Singing–Instruction and study. 2. Musicals–Instruction and study. I. Title.
MT956.H34 2014
782.1'143–dc23
2013048847

♾TM The paper used in this publication meets the minimum requirements of American National Standard for Information Sciences Permanence of Paper for Printed Library Materials, ANSI/NISO Z39.48-1992.

Printed in the United States of America

Dedicated to the three wonderful women who encouraged, supported, loved, and made me who I am today. I
want to acknowledge the huge difference they made in
my life.

Sandra Otts Hall, mother

Jessie McKinney Otts, grandmother

Jean Nicolas, first voice teacher (high school)

CONTENTS

LIST OF FIGURES

ACKNOWLEDGMENTS

Rarely is any endeavor a solo pursuit. Writing this book is no exception. I would like to thank Allen Henderson, executive editor of this series and executive director of the National Association of Teachers of Singing for his always kind and helpful advice; Wayne Lee, my writing coach for helping me improve my work immeasurably; Mary Saunders-Barton for her support and friendship; Bennett Graff, senior acquisitions editor at Rowman & Littlefield for challenging me to improve my work; and all my friends and family who offered their words of support along the way.

FOREWORD

If you are holding this book in your hands, you were prompted by the title. Possibly you are a classical singer or performer considering a trip to the dark side, or a music theater performer who has felt adrift in terms of technique because you never connected to a teacher who addressed your concerns. Whatever your motivation, this book will give you the courage to pursue proficiency in the wonderful art of music theater singing.

For many reasons, Karen Hall is the perfect choice to write this book. She has taken the very same journey many of you are charting, and it is what gives her the credentials to lead you forward. She, like many people smitten by music theater in their early years, became a classical singer when no other option seemed available. Times have changed!

I first met Karen at the National Association of Teachers of Singing (NATS) winter workshop in New York City in 2000. During a session I taught called "Sing Out, Louise!" she jubilantly experimented with her own belt. She has since been actively teaching and researching the style and building an impressive knowledge base to bring to this book.

It's a daunting project, but Karen has undertaken it with energy and passion. By definition, music theater is a collaborative art form, incorporating a host of different skills. Music theater singing teachers depend on the support of their colleagues in voice science, health matters, and real-world performance practice. Karen has very wisely realized that no single person could write this book, and she has enlisted the help of experts in these key areas to augment and strengthen the work.

A strong additional feature will be a listening component. How can you be sure of sounds without actually hearing them? The book is organized to give you the maximum opportunity to comprehend technical differences between classical and music theater singing, and the aural factor is critical to that.

A number of years ago, it would have seemed unthinkable to legitimize a pedagogy considered not only alternative but also possibly dangerous to the voice. The only way Broadway performers could work on the kind of singing they were being asked to do was on their own by trial and error or in a private New York City studio with a teacher who honored the style. Sometimes even those teachers hesitated to encourage students to make sounds they could not make themselves.

Times have changed! As someone hopelessly in love with this art form, I am deeply gratified to see a book on music theater singing finally available to take its place beside the mountain of resources at hand for classical singers. It's a mighty first step!

Mary Saunders-Barton
Head of Voice for Music Theatre
Head of Graduate Voice Pedagogy for Music Theatre
Penn State University

INTRODUCTION

When I was a little girl, I fell in love with music, especially voice and piano. Whether it was in church, at pop music concerts, on TV, or at music theater productions such as *South Pacific*, *My Fair Lady*, and *Mary Poppins*, I always came away humming the songs. I was hooked. I wanted to be up there onstage, singing those songs, playing the leading roles in those shows.

When I was eight, my mother enrolled me in private piano lessons; a few years later, I started studying voice as well. I learned all the tunes from all those musicals on the piano and sang along for hours on end. In high school, I joined the chorus, continued my private lessons, and studied selections from both the music theater and classical repertoires. Still hooked, I majored in voice at college.

I was thrilled to be pursuing my music theater dream—but there was one big problem: the only singing courses offered at my university were in classical voice production. There was just no way to major in music theater. While my classical education gave me a love of classical music, and I don't regret any of my classical education, sadly, I left behind my music theater aspirations and earned my degrees in classical voice. After graduation, I performed professionally in several music theater productions, but most of my performance experience since that time has been in the classical genres.

That is why I wrote this book.

In a way, I wrote *So You Want to Sing Music Theater* for that disappointed college student whose music theater hopes seemed like an impossible dream. Like me, you have probably had difficulty finding a teacher or instructional materials that address your specific vocal needs. So this book is for all of you who want to sing or teach music theater performance as it should be sung or taught: by, and for, music theater professionals.

So, why me, why now?

I was asked to write this book for an innovative and important series being published by Rowman & Littlefield because of the music theater singing research I conducted as part of my doctoral studies. I was also asked because I am a singer and voice teacher, not merely an academician. Finally, music theater singing is one of my great passions in life. I could not resist helping launch a vocal series project the likes of which has never been attempted until now—a series that includes all styles of singing. All I can say is *it's about time!*

In 1991, when I began teaching at the university level, I taught applied classical voice. Several years later, I was hired to teach at the Boston Conservatory, and as a new instructor, I was "required" to teach all music theater majors. This was a crossroads experience. These students were using terms and making sounds outside of my teaching and performing experience. They also had a different personal energy than the classical students I was used to teaching.

I was challenged, and also intrigued.

I resisted my impulse to impose a classical technique. Instead, I decided to do what any good teacher does: learn from my students. For the most part, the sounds they were making were healthy but certainly not sounds I was used to hearing in classical singing. These young women and men were singing in the mix/belt style. They told me they had learned this technique either from a high school teacher or, more often, had just figured it out on their own.

Clearly, classical vocal technique, vocabulary, and repertoire were for the most part not appropriate for these students. Furthermore, there were no instructional materials available to help me transition from teaching classical to music theater singing. I had no choice but to adapt my teaching methods. Through trial and error, I developed ways of teaching these music theater vocal techniques, figured out the appropriate repertoire for the multitude of styles that these students needed to master, and developed a new vocabulary to teach music theater singing and styles. There are many ways to achieve a healthy music theater singing sound, I discovered, and teachers need to honor these diverse approaches if they are to be successful in helping students prepare for careers in music theater.

During my second year at the conservatory, I began to pursue a doctoral degree in education. As I pondered a dissertation topic, it occurred to me that there was an enormous need for an introductory guide for teaching music theater vocal pedagogy and styles.

Students pursuing music theater vocal study are expected to sing repertoire in virtually every style found in music theater history. This range, from classical to rock and even rhythm and blues, is evidenced by the current shows on Broadway. For example, during the 2012–2013 Broadway season, the classically oriented production of Rodgers and Hammerstein's *Cinderella*, the rock production of *Rock of Ages*, and rhythm and blues based *Motown: The Musical* were playing simultaneously. Many voice teachers and singers have begun to classify any type of nonclassical singing as contemporary commercial music (CCM). The categories included in CCM include the entire range of styles found in music theater: cabaret, country, experimental, folk, gospel, jazz, rock, pop, rap, rhythm and blues, and, of course, "legit" music theater.

There is still much research needed on mix/belt (CCM) singing. For instance, while conducting my doctoral research, I did not find any studies about the male belt voice. Even more confusing is the fact that the scientific and teaching communities have not even been able to agree on a general definition of belt singing. With that said, I can only hope that, when it finally is defined, the "definition" is broad and inclusive enough to encompass the entire spectrum of music theater styles.

The diversity of those styles gives rise to a much more individualistic and idiosyncratic sound than is found among classical singers. In fact, some studies have shown that it is actually the singer's uniqueness of sound and approach, rather than their mastery of any one prototypical sound, that causes casting directors to hire one singer over another.

As the vocal demands and popularity of music theater singing continue to grow, the study, understanding, and teaching of music theater singing have begun to evolve to meet those demands. With the advent and growth of voice science, our understanding of how music theater singing is both similar to and different from classical singing has skyrocketed. Many outmoded ideas about music theater singing have (thank goodness!) been patently disproven. Now we know that mix/belt singing is not wrong, unhealthy, undesirable, nor inferior to classical technique, as many voice teachers have so ardently proclaimed over the years. And now that the genre itself is becoming more widely accepted, music theater singers finally have their own customized tools for learning to sing healthily—and proudly—in the music theater style.

Those tools are waiting for you to discover in this book.

The topics in these pages constitute an overview of all aspects of singing music theater selections, including the characteristics of the music theater style, the techniques necessary to sing the associated selections, the history of the genre, the related voice science and health issues, and the performance aspects of working with music theater coaches, teachers, and conductors. Audio and visual examples that support the text will help you hear the sounds being discussed, the sounds you want to make when you sing music theater songs.

The book is intended for all ages and levels of singers, from beginner to professional. It can also be used as a resource for voice teachers, vocal coaches, and conductors to support their teaching. For beginning singers, it will function as a comprehensive learning guide to singing music theater songs; for more advanced singers, it will serve as a review and also bring you up to speed on what is new and evolving. Whatever your level, expertise, or job description, this book will deepen your understanding of how you sing and expose you to current trends, procedures, and expectations in the field.

If there had been a music theater degree offered when I attended college, I most likely would have enrolled in such a program and happily spent my career performing music theater. But then I might not have ended up writing this book. *So You Want to Sing Music Theater* is an outgrowth from, and an extension of, my life's work, and I am honored to be the author. May you use it in good voice!

Many of the musical examples cited in this book, as well as other books in this series, are freely available on the Internet. All supplemental materials for this book can be found at www.SoYouWantToSing.org.

HISTORY OF MUSIC THEATER

The most appropriate place to begin learning how to sing in the music theater style is with a basic understanding of the background and history of the genre. Given that the American musical is a uniquely American form, and that music theater performances on Broadway are attracting record crowds (12.3 million in 2012), that understanding takes on even more importance (Fandemonium, 2012).

HISTORICAL PERSPECTIVE

Music theater history teaches you how all the composers are "connected," how their composition techniques and styles influenced those that came after them. This knowledge is essential to your performance practices. For instance, some music, composers, and styles are performed exactly as notated on the page. Other composers expect the vocal line to be "taken off the page," a technique also called "back phrasing." Contemporary composers Stephen Sondheim and Robert Jason Brown expect you to sing what's on the page. Many other contemporary music theater composers do not. The historical perspective teaches you this important distinction and much more. Composers and the compositional choices they have made throughout music theater history also determine how a song is sung. Some universities have begun to develop and add a historical thread or timeline into music classes. In all likelihood, a twenty-year-old won't naturally gravitate toward connecting music history issues to the music, but I challenge you to add this important component to your learning experience. It is an essential element of your music theater education.

Despite its current popularity, music theater mix/belt singing is not new. Many consider the female music theater mix/belt voice an American vocal technique that emerged on music theater stages in the early nineteenth century (Green, 1980; Roll 2012). Mix/belt singing is more speech-oriented, and it allows female voices to project unamplified in the middle register (C_4–C_5), the register that coincides with the female speaking voice range. "By the 1980s and 1990s, the belt sound was the dominant vocal style used for females in musicals" (Roll, 2012, 6). During the past fifteen years, an even newer approach to music theater singing has emerged based on the popularity of the pop/rock style musical. The "legit" style of singing isn't a part of the pop/rock singing style, giving even more prominence to the use of the mix/belt singing voice. During 2012, fourteen of the twenty-five musicals on Broadway were written in the pop/rock style (Roll, 2012).

The earliest American musicals of the eighteenth and nineteenth centuries were mostly derived from much older European ancestral forms: opera, operetta, vaudeville, extravaganza, variety, burlesque, and minstrel shows. Even the contemporary shows of today owe a debt to those precursors and exhibit a wide range and mixture of all those styles, along with more modern styles such as pop, rock, rhythm and blues, and jazz. Music theater is nothing if not diverse—in both its music and styles of singing. This combination of styles, both vocal and musical, has created a musical melting pot of sorts, reflecting the multiethnic population shifts that have taken place throughout the history of the United States.

The history of music theater in America encompasses several main periods of gradual growth, as it took many years for the American musical as we have come to know it to find its own identity, rather than merely mimicking the European forms (Lubbock, 1962). This next section explores the historic connections between music theater and its European roots, along with a look at how more modern innovations gave rise to current music theater singing and styles.

1735–1864: THE EARLY PIONEERS

Extravaganza, pantomime, variety, and the minstrel show were the prevailing types of entertainment in this early era (Smith and Litton, 1950), and all contributed to the evolution of the modern-day American musical. That evolution has not always been smooth, though. The Dutch population in New York City, for example, considered theater sinful, so professional theater performances did not regularly appear there until the 1730s (Kenrick, 2009). It wasn't until 1750 that *The Beggar's Opera*, widely regarded as the first American play to be performed with music, opened at New York City's Nassau Street Theater, performed by the traveling troupe of Walter Murray and Thomas Kean (Kenrick, 2009).

The first musical production in the United States actually occurred much earlier, though—on February 8, 1735, in fact. And that production, an English ballad opera called *Flora*, was staged in a Charleston, South Carolina, courtroom (Lubbock, 1962). A ballad opera is a comic play containing popular ballads set with new lyrics satirizing current events and personalities (Kenrick, 2009).

"The American Revolution had a crippling effect on all forms of theatre," writes John Kenrick in his *Musical Theatre: A History*. In addition, the new U.S. government, the Continental Congress, approved a resolution opposing theater productions, and the states soon responded by passing laws outlawing all stage performances. Those laws remained intact from 1780 until 1793. It wasn't until after they were rescinded that stage productions gradually began to reappear, supported in part by President George Washington's regular theater attendance. Still, the American stage continued to rely mostly on imported forms such as British plays and European comic opera (Kenrick, 2009). Truly American musicals started to appear in the 1790s, but the older forms remained more popular for some time to come.

"The earliest American musicals were comic operas[—]satirical operas with original scores and libretti" (Kenrick, 2009). The decade ended with a growth spurt of wide-ranging musical productions in New York City, with most theatrical performances of the time including musical numbers of some type. Straight plays would often include musical numbers between acts, and even some performances of Shakespearean tragedies were known to have included popular songs or musical numbers as pre-play "curtain risers," between acts, or as a post-performance "after piece" (Kenrick, 2009).

During the early 1800s in New York City, Broadway was the hub of the American theater; consequently, all the best businesses and theaters wanted to be located there. The population of the city was expanding and becoming more diverse, and the popularity of theater was on the rise. Melodrama, romances, and burletta were the most popular musical forms during this time. Melodramas contained simple, good-versus-evil plots fueled by dramatic background music, popular songs, and grandiose stage effects. Romances were original musical works based on the comic opera style, but the subject matter was more sentimental in nature. "The term 'burletta' was originally used to describe a comic opera that burlesqued popular topics, but applied to almost any dramatic production that included songs" (Kenrick, 2009).

Racial Barriers

William Henry Brown (a Black West Indian and former ship's steward) opened a "pleasure garden" in his New York City backyard during the summer of 1821. His pleasure garden was the first Black-owned entertainment venue in New York City to open its doors to African American audiences (Kenrick, 2009). Since Blacks were not allowed to attend any theaters in town, Brown attracted full houses and soon expanded into the American Theatre on Mercer Street. His all-Black productions used the same format of plays and musical acts found in White theaters, and soon began drawing curious White theatergoers (Kenrick, 2009).

At first, Brown's success was tolerated by officials and regarded with humor by the newspapers. "However, when he had the audacity to lease a performance space on Broadway, the establishment reacted with alarm" (Kenrick, 2009). At trial a White judge ruled that Brown's Negro company was banned from any future performances of Shakespeare (Kenrick, 2009). Even though Brown obeyed the court ruling and returned to his old location, the harassment continued and forced him to close his doors by 1823. "African-American performers would not return to the legitimate stage until after the Civil War, and all-Black productions would not successfully return to Broadway until the next century" (Kenrick, 2009).

Unfortunately, anti-Black prejudice did not stop the creation and increasing popularity of the minstrel show, a new variety entertainment form based on the denigration of African American culture (Kenrick, 2009). The minstrel show attracted mostly White audiences by exploiting with racist "humor" the dance, song, and traditions of the African American culture. Minstrel shows, one of the most popular music theater forms of the early era, crystallized and gained widespread popularity beginning in 1842–1843, when a group of four unemployed blackface circus performers created a full-length blackface routine (Kenrick, 2009). "Calling themselves *The Virginia Minstrels* (spoofing the popular Tyrolese Minstrels of Switzerland), their 'plantation songs' and shuffling dances caused a sensation" (Kenrick, 2009). Minstrel companies soon toured the country inspired by the four-man blackface troupe. New York City audiences supported the minstrel show for about twenty-five years, but the genre was kept alive by numerous troupes that toured and entertained the smaller cities and towns throughout the United States well into the twentieth century (Kenrick, 2003). After the Civil War, minstrel shows were the only performance outlet available to African American performers. Regrettably, the minstrel show is historically significant because it was the first American-born form of music theater, influencing all future Black musicals (Kenrick, 2003).

Laura Keene

Meanwhile, New York City's expanding and increasingly sophisticated population was creating a demand for grander and more sophisticated types of entertainments. Riding the momentum of this new cultural wave, Laura Keene was one of the first women to find national success and name recognition as an actress in and manager of her own troupe. Her production of *The Elves* (1857) set the record as Broadway's first "long-run" musical with a run of fifty performances and was followed by an even more astonishing achievement—her "musical burletta" *The Seven Sisters* (1860) racked up an unprecedented 253-performance run. Keene and seven other women starred as female demons "that come up from hell to go sightseeing in New York. With its bold blend of patriotic fantasy, spectacular sets, and a 'transformation scene' (where the entire stage set changed in full view of the audience), *Seven Sisters* was a clear precursor to the more widely remembered hits that followed later that decade" (Kenrick, 2009).

The Civil War

While the Civil War (1861–1865) was waged, most theater productions were produced in the North because of the bigger populations and wealth. During the war, actors were given clearance to perform for audiences on both sides of the conflict. When the war ended, and after a brief financial panic in New York City, audiences adjusted and quickly rebuilt. Audiences sought out entertainment that distracted them from the war and its ravages. During the war, musical fantasies (*Cinderella*) and burlesques poking fun at the current events of the day (*King Cotton*) were the musical forms most popular with audiences. Laura Keene and her repertory company staged eight musicals. In 1863 Keene and her troupe began touring with the eight shows because she was forced, due to financial difficulties, to close her New York City theater. "Sadly, Keene is mainly remembered because President Abraham Lincoln was assassinated in 1865 while watching her performance in the popular comedy *Our American Cousin* at Ford's Theatre in Washington, D.C." (Kenrick, 2009).

1865–1919: PRECURSORS OF THE GOLDEN AGE

The close of the Civil War brought about a time of uncommon redefinition for the young nation. The musical stage, of course, was part of the redefining process. In 1866 two major events marked the start of changing times for the American theater. The first event occurred in early 1866 when *The Black Domino/Between You, Me and the Post*, a Broadway double bill, called itself a musical comedy. No score or libretto survives, but the use of the term "musical comedy" signaled important change. The second important theatrical event, a production of *The Black Crook*, occurred later in 1866 and has been called "the first Broadway musical" by some. Unfortunately, that is not true, but it was "America's first *bona fide* nationwide musical blockbuster" (Kenrick, 2009).

The roots of the early American musical are found in the time period of approximately 1865 to 1919. This era is characterized by reviews, vaudeville acts, burlesque, and productions of imported European operetta by composers Johann Strauss (1825–1899) and Jacques Offenbach (1819–1880), a genre featuring the text. Impresario Florenz Ziegfeld was a prominent vaudeville producer, and his opulent productions were known for lavish costumes and beautiful showgirls. Irving Berlin arrived on Broadway in 1914 after years of writing for Yiddish theater. A few of the notable performers of this era were Al Jolson, Eddie Cantor, Bert Lahr, Jimmy Durante, Beatrice Lillie, Fanny Brice, and Gertrude Lawrence. Many vaudeville performers also performed on live radio shows. Radio show singing was speech-oriented and served as another early influence on the speech approach to singing used in music theater today.

The Industrial Revolution

By the 1880s, the face of rural America had been changed by the Industrial Revolution. With half of the population living in towns or cities and working at regulated jobs, they found themselves with free time and extra money—luxuries they never had in rural America. As a result, they wanted regular and affordable entertainment. Phonographs, film, radio, and television did not yet exist, but vaudeville helped fill the gap. It is unclear where the term *vaudeville* developed, although some claim the word was crudely derived from the French "voix de ville," slang for "songs of the town." Others believe the source was the satirical song "Vaux de Vire" by Olivier Basselin. Whatever the derivation, by 1907 vaudeville acts were earning a combined $30 million a year. The more affordable ticket price of a vaudeville show was a major reason they attracted larger audiences than the major Broadway productions, whose admission was often 25 percent higher. In 1912, a survey found that some seven hundred thousand New Yorkers attended vaudeville productions *each week*. The working class (mostly men) made up nearly two-thirds of that number, compared to a mere 2 percent who attended Broadway shows (Kenrick, 2004).

Vaudeville Performers

Performing in a vaudeville act was challenging and strenuous because successful acts toured for at least forty weeks a year. Salaries, however, were a key motivator: performers, even those with smaller roles, were paid at least three times the average weekly salary of a factory worker. More than twenty-five thousand people performed in the fifty-plus years of vaudeville history. Performances were divided into levels: "small time," "medium time," and "big time." The theaters and salaries improved with each level, ranging from crude, small town theaters, which served as training grounds for newer performers, to the finer theaters in the biggest cities. Small time performer salaries ranged from fifteen to seventy dollars a week, whereas big time performers were paid up to $1,000 a week. Anyone with enough determination and talent could earn a very good living as a vaudeville performer (Kenrick, 2004).

Burlesque Musicals

The first burlesque musicals appeared in the United States in the 1840s. After the Colonies had banded together to form the United States, the interest in burlesque became more popular. "At the time, burlesque consisted of travesties on or parodies of famous plays, performers, or dancers—in song, dance pantomime, and dialogue," writes Mark Lubbock in *The Complete Book of Light Opera* (1962). Still, however, burlesque represented an imported European form, known (and popular) for emphasizing females in flimsy attire, a characteristic still present in many modern-day American musicals. They were lavish, full-length British imports that poked fun at the operas, books, and plays enjoyed by the upper class. A hint of sex appeal was also an important element. These burlesque musicals were intended for short runs, and then they disappeared. One of the most important and lasting influences of the early burlesque musicals was the establishment of women on stage. Sometimes women even played both the male and female roles. Often the women were dressed in what was considered at the time revealing clothing, most specifically tights. "Proper" women of the day kept their bodies hidden and covered beneath bustles, lace, and modest hemlines. "The very sight of a female body not covered by accepted costume of bourgeois respectability forcefully if playfully called attention to the entire question of the 'place' of wom[e]n in American society," writes John Kenrick (2003).

Not surprisingly, Broadway soon created an American version of the imported British burlesque musicals, often described as burlesque extravaganzas. Complete with lavish staging, special effects, and opulent costumes, the comedic focus was often multifaceted, lampooning everyone and everything from famous persons to popular books, popular culture, and more. Edward Rice, the most important composer and producer of this era, produced numerous burlesque musicals on Broadway, as well as many tours throughout the United States. Rice also composed original music for all his scores. In an 1893 interview, he described the difference between a burlesque musical and extravaganza: "An extravaganza permits any extravagances or whimsicalities, without definite purpose. A burlesque should burlesque something. It should be pregnant with meaning. It should be pure, wholesome, free from suggestiveness. It should fancifully and humorously distort fact. It should have consistency of plot, idealization of treatment in effects of scenery and costumes, fantastic drollery of movement and witchery of musical embellishment. It should be performed by comedians who understand the value of light and shade, and the sharp accenting of every salient point" (Kenrick, 2003). Burlesque musicals lasted through the 1890s.

Gilbert and Sullivan

In the 1870s, British playwright William Gilbert and British composer Arthur Sullivan began their famous collaboration that forever changed the landscape of music theater in both England and America. Their comedic, melodic operettas set a new standard for composition and professionalism. In Britain during the 1860s, the most popular forms of music theater had been variety shows, French operettas, and comic light operas. Gilbert and Sullivan changed all that—particularly their groundbreaking *HMS Pinafore*. Stateside, an unauthorized version of the play caused the craze known as "Pinafore-Mania." Gilbert and Sullivan's works continued their popularity in the United States through the twentieth century and continue to be frequently performed today. Many American lyricists credit the work of Gilbert as a heavy influence on their work—Larry Hart, Allen Jay Lerner, and Stephen Sondheim, to name a few. American audiences quickly lost interest in the other available forms of entertainment and chose instead to attend operetta performances by Gilbert and Sullivan. This caused the standards of stage work in the United States to change and improve, thus making way for the new and more ambitious American musicals yet to be written.

The Black Crook

The Black Crook, written by playwright Charles M. Barras, opened on September 12, 1866, at Niblo's Garden, one of Manhattan's most popular theaters. William Wheatley produced it, with music by George Bickwell and choreography by David Costa. The show ran a total of 475 performances before closing on January 4, 1868. *The Black Crook* is often referred to as the first American musical, even though it was actually an extravaganza that combined the French Romantic ballet and the German Romantic melodrama. The pairing of the French and German forms came about only because of a fire that destroyed New York's Academy of Music; suddenly, promoters Henry Jarrett and Harry Palmer found themselves with a Parisian ballet troupe and a cargo load full of sets but nowhere to perform. Meanwhile, William Wheatley, manager and sometimes actor of Niblo's Garden, struck a deal with the promoters Jarrett and Palmer, and the "big time" Broadway musical was born. The opening night performance lasted five and a half hours! *The Black Crook* went on to run for 474 performances and grossed over a million dollars during its yearlong run—success that was aided, no doubt, by the controversial inclusion of a female chorus (starring prima ballerina Marie Bonfanti) dressed in flesh-colored tights (Kenrick, 2003).

"The scenery and the legs are everything; the actors who do the talking are the wretchedest sticks on the boards," wrote Mark Twain after seeing a production in 1867. "But the fairy scenes—they fascinate the boys! Beautiful bare-legged girls hanging in flower baskets; others stretched in groups on great sea shells; others clustered around fluted columns; . . . all lit up with gorgeous theatrical fires, and witnessed through a great gauzy curtain that counterfeits a soft silver mist! It is the wonders of the Arabian Nights realized" (1867).

The Mulligan Guard Picnic

Twelve years later, in 1878, *The Mulligan Guard Picnic* opened, an expanded vaudeville sketch with dialogue, costumes, and music. The show was part of a larger series of musicals called the *Mulligan Guard* series, produced and written by Americans Ed Harrigan and Tony Hart, who also starred in the series. "The format was the European burlesque and extravaganza, but the material was completely American," writes Mark Lubbock in *The complete book of light opera* (1962).

The singing in the entertainment genres of the 1880s highlighted the text, and until amplification was added to the theater stage in the late 1920s and 1930s, the only way a singer could expect to be heard by audience members was to "belt it out." "The history of the sound we associate with the word 'belting,' the pedagogical term used to describe a majority of the singing timbre found in music theater, goes back a long way," writes Jeannette LoVetri (LoVetri, 2013, 4). "It can be found all over the world—in African music from many countries, in Flamenco from Spain, in Mariachi from Mexico, in Middle Eastern music, particularly in religious application. In the United States it can be found not only in music theater but gospel, country, pop, and rock music" (LoVetri, 2013, 4).

Pantomime

Pantomime acts tell a story with body or facial movements, and these one acts were usually paired with other types of entertainment beginning in the 1700s on both the London and Broadway stages. American pantomime often took characters from Mother Goose stories and transformed them, via a magic fairy, into clown figures from the Italian commedia dell' arte. Consequently, pantomime is sometimes described as "children's theater for adults." Using silent gestures to convey the mostly comedic stories, the clowns were known to suddenly start singing to advance the plot or increase audience excitement. Many in the audience of the day were immigrants and spoke little English, so with the aid of pantomime they did not miss dialogue in a language they barely understood or spoke. Pantomime was no longer part of the American stage by 1880, though, because "audiences wanted something more intimate than burlesque and less childish than pantomime. The time was right for an innovation—the form we now know as musical comedy" (Kenrick, 2003).

MUSICALS BY DECADE

1920–1930

The 1920s was a time of remarkable artistic development in the music theater genre; it was Broadway's busiest decade, with some seasons introducing as many as fifty new music theater productions. Some musicologists suggest that the "Golden Age" of Broadway began in 1925 when four blockbusters by Vincent Youmans, Rudolf Friml, Jerome Kern, and Richard Rodgers and Lorenz Hart opened within a span of seven days. With the founding of ASCAP (the American Society of Composers, Authors, and Publishers) in 1924, American composers now had the ability to protect their intellectual property. The musical revue *Shuffle Along* (1921), produced, written, and performed by African Americans, was one of the longest-running musicals of the time, so popular it caused "curtain time traffic jams" on Sixty-third Street. Flournoy Miller and Aubrey Lyles wrote it, with lyrics by Noble Sissle and Eubie Blake, and it launched the careers of Josephine Baker, Paul Robeson, and Adelaide Hall (Kenrick, 2003).

The most important marker of this decade was the 1927 production of *Showboat* by composer Jerome Kern and lyricist-librettist Oscar Hammerstein II. This show was revolutionary in two ways: it depicted a political (racial) issue, and it was the first "book" musical. In a book musical, the script tells a story and the songs are written to continue or embellish the dramatic situation. Previously, theatrical shows were put together as a series of unrelated songs that interrupted the dramatic action and often had nothing to do with the plot. The book musical became the dominant music theater genre (and remains an important model today), though the older styles previously mentioned continued to be produced during this decade: the Ziegfeld Follies, revues, and some vaudeville, though it was rapidly being replaced by burlesque.

Some of the greatest Broadway composers were writing and producing musicals during this decade: Rodgers and Hart, George and Ira Gershwin, Vincent Youmans, Jerome Kern, Cole Porter, and Irving Berlin, to name a few. Sigmund Romberg, Rudolf Friml, and Emmerich Kalman were composing operettas. The premiere star of the music theater stage during this time, Al Jolson, was born in Russia in 1886. For more than forty years, he was known in the industry as "the World's Greatest Entertainer" (Ciolino, 2013). The "Golden Age" bubble had to burst, though, and with the stock market crash of 1929, tough times lay ahead for Broadway.

1930–1940

In the early part of the decade, many shows were still rooted in opera, operetta, and vaudeville. In 1932, the last vaudeville show closed its doors, and "some feared a similar fate was in store for the Broadway musical" (Kenrick, 2003). The Great Depression was in full force, with many Americans going without jobs, housing, or even enough to eat. But the nationwide chain of theaters owned by the Shubert brothers of New York City helped save the day. Back in 1924, the Shuberts ran eighty-six theaters in the United States alone, controlling 60 percent of the legitimate theater in the country, producing a quarter of all American plays, and raking in $1 million a week in ticket sales. They also owned their own ticket brokerage, a voice/dance school, and huge tracts of real estate (pbs.org). By 1931, though, their empire had crumbled, and the Shuberts declared bankruptcy. They escaped dissolution, however, by repurchasing the properties at auction and segueing into a new company called Select Theatre Corporation. Their business savvy is one of the main reasons theater in the United States survived the Depression (shubertarchive.org).

In spite of the financial hardship caused by the Depression, the Broadway musical continued to reach new artistic heights. The 1930s is an important era in music theater because many prominent composers found their voice and their audience. Many of the songs of Porter, Berlin, Kern, and Harold Arlen were written during this decade, and their songs remain some of the most popular and well-known songs of today. George and Ira Gershwin produced six musicals and gave Broadway the milestone jazz opera *Porgy and Bess* (1935). For this show, which chronicled the life of poor Blacks in the fishing village of Catfish Row, South Carolina, the Gershwins collaborated with writers DuBose and Dorothy Heyward, who wrote the original novel and adapted the play for the stage (Kenrick, 2003). The score was a unique blend of classical, popular, and jazz styles expressing indescribable pathos and passionate joy amid abject poverty.

After an unsuccessful venture in Hollywood, Richard Rodgers and Lorenzo Hart returned to Broadway with several music theater successes in the decade (*Jumbo, On Your Toes, Babes in Arms*, to name a few). During the 1930s, the revue was still popular but experienced a dramatic change in form. Bigger (read: Ziegfeld Follies) was no longer better, and the old formula had lost its public appeal. Instead, composers produced much stronger scores and visually stunning productions, and they proved popular with audiences. The most successful Broadway composer during the 1930s was Cole Porter, who had more hit shows than any other composer during this time. Porter also wrote for film, but his music theater compositions were considered "state of the art." During the 1930s, Ethel Merman rose to stardom as a belter. Her popularity was due, in large part, to the fact that her voice projected throughout the theater without the use of a microphone.

1940–1950

As the decade began, the lingering effects of the Depression and the ominous lead-up to World War II convinced most producers that audiences wanted a night of light entertainment and cheerful songs to escape the realities of the day. Revues were actually rare on Broadway in the 1940s, though, due in large part to the popularity of free nightly all-star variety entertainment on the radio. As it turns out, the producers underestimated their audience. Since 1911, Irving Berlin had been the most popular composer in America, with numerous contributions to film and stage revues. The successful team of Rodgers and Hart now became Rodgers and Hammerstein due to Hart's ongoing battle with alcoholism. Their first book musical, *Louisiana Purchase*, was produced in 1940. Their 1943 production of *Oklahoma!* marks another turning point in music theater history. The dramatic use of ballet by choreographer Agnes de Mille, the realistic Midwestern story, the beautiful music, and the amalgamation of all elements with the book were all innovations in the creation of a music theater work. The show was neither a musical nor an operetta; instead, it was something new, a musical play where all the elements existed to develop the characters and story. Suddenly, a new benchmark had been set: Broadway composers now had to become dramatists, not just tunesmiths. Rodgers and Hammerstein also created another long-lasting favorite during this decade, *Carousel*. Cole Porter and Irving Berlin successfully answered the challenge with *Kiss Me Kate* (considered the best score of Porter's career) and *Annie Get Your Gun*, starring Ethel Merman in her longest-running role.

Kurt Weill also began composing musicals during the 1940s that blurred the line between music theater and opera, most notably *Threepenny Opera*. The use of the German innovation of *Sprechstimme* by Weill, in some of his compositions, was another example of how musicals and opera were similar. *Sprechstimme* translates as "speak/voice" and results in an emphasis on the enunciation of text rather than on beauty of sound and resonance. Meanwhile, operettas were still being written and performed, and new composers such as Frank Loesser, Jules Styne, Lerner and Loewe, and Betty Comden and Adolph Green were making a name for themselves. Singer/dancers Gene Kelly and Mary Martin rose to stardom, and fears of the impending World War II were reflected in the last musical hit of the decade, Rodgers and Hammerstein's *South Pacific*, which gave Americans not only memorable songs, but confronted them with their bigotries and racial prejudice.

1950–1960

The 1950s produced some of the most popular and frequently performed shows of today, composing the core of the music theater repertory. These shows were—and still are—a prominent part of American popular culture. This decade is considered the height of the "Golden Age" in music theater, and the shows of this era are referred to as "traditional." The style of "legit" singing was prominent during this time. *The King and I, Wonderful Town, My Fair Lady, The Pajama Game*, and *West Side Story* are a few examples of the bountiful output during this decade.

Rodgers and Hammerstein continued their creative output during the 1950s: *The King and I* (1951), *Me and Juliet* (1953), *Pipe Dream* (1955), *Flower Drum Song* (1958), and in 1959, *The Sound of Music* opened, a still-beloved cultural landmark. Unfortunately, a few months after the opening night of *The Sound of Music*, Oscar Hammerstein died. "More than any other individual, Hammerstein turned the Broadway musical into a potent dramatic form, and turned lyrics into essential dramatic tools," writes Kenrick. "He did it by being a superb storyteller and a dedicated craftsman" (Kenrick, 2004).

Rodgers and Hammerstein weren't the only composers and lyricists producing dynamic shows in the 1950s. In spite of suffering crippling injuries to both legs in a horse-riding accident in 1937 that resulted in more than thirty operations over twenty years, Cole Porter produced some of his funniest songs and shows, including *Can Can* (1953) and *Silk Stockings* (1955). Frank Loesser's composer-lyricist versatility was unmatched during his day. His landmark creation, *Guys and Dolls* (1950), is considered by some to be the greatest musical ever written. As a testament to his versatility, Loesser also wrote the opera *The Most Happy Fella* (1956). Harold Rome was a standout for his comedic songs; Irving Berlin concentrated his efforts in Hollywood; and popular radio program music director Meredith Willson spent years writing and refining his masterpiece, *The Music Man* (1957), and later the hugely popular *The Unsinkable Molly Brown* (1960) (Kenrick, 2003).

Barbara Cook appeared as Marian the librarian in Willson's *The Music Man,* a role that earned her the title of Broadway's premier ingénue of the day. Lerner and Loewe enjoyed a modest success with *Paint Your Wagon* (1951) and surprised many when they announced plans to stage George Bernard Shaw's comedy *Pygmalion.* Many scoffed at the idea and said it couldn't be done, and even the genius Oscar Hammerstein was wrong in his prediction that the project wouldn't work. *My Fair Lady* (1956) opened to unanimous rave reviews, won all the major awards, became the longest-running musical of the day, and featured leading lady Julie Andrews. *My Fair Lady* is also often described as the greatest musical theater work ever written, filled with uncanny story/song integration, heart, and beautiful melodies. Lerner and Loewe finished out the decade with their production of *Camelot* (1960), another smash hit featuring Andrews, along with Richard Burton. Lastly, the huge talent and charisma of conductor and composer Leonard Bernstein gave the Broadway stage some of the most ambitious scores of the time by blending classical, pop, and jazz styles in his unique voice that has been described as quintessential New York City. The three musicals he wrote during this time, all major hits, featured New York: *Wonderful Town* (1953), *Candide* (1956), and *West Side Story* (1957).

1960–1970

The early, middle, and late eras of the 1960s are each marked by an important historical event. In 1960, the longest-running Off-Broadway musical (*The Fantastiks*) opened and went on to play for more than four decades. Another popular hit of the early 1960s, *Bye Bye Birdie* (1960), featured youthful themes and was perhaps an accidental precursor to the explosion of counterculture rock elements waiting to explode onto the Broadway stage. In the mid-1960s, the Golden Age on Broadway quietly ended. Several very successful musicals opened during this last phase of the Golden Age and ran for over a thousand performances—an unprecedented record number: *Hello Dolly* (1964), *Funny Girl* (1964), *Fiddler on the Roof* (1964), *Man of La Mancha* (1965), *Fame* (1966), and *Cabaret* (1966).

The cultural upheaval of the late 1960s also brought the beginnings of monumental change to the Broadway stage and behind the scenes. A chasm was created between the culture of "drugs, sex, and rock 'n' roll" and the "establishment" of the time, and the hard rock sound of popular music was demanding its place on the Broadway stage. The late 1960s are important because of the introduction of experimental and innovative rock 'n' roll music theater productions. The most well-known and influential rock musical was the 1968 production of *Hair*. Even though Tony voters ignored it, others such as *The New York Times* critic Clive Barnes used the power of the pen to praise *Hair* as "the first Broadway musical in some time to have the authentic voice of today" (Kenrick, 2003). The decade ended with the contradictions of the times reflected in the fact that *Hello Dolly* and *Fiddler on the Roof*, war horses of the previous era, still enjoyed long runs, while the newer composers were searching for how and what to write next. The Broadway musical wasn't dead, but it was in a state of transition.

1970–1980

Productions in this decade continued to be experimental, with a tug of war for dominance between rock musicals, "concept" shows, and conventional post-*Oklahoma*-type musicals. Rock musicals, such as *Godspell* (1971), *Jesus Christ Superstar* (1971), and *Grease* (1972), continued to be popular, alongside more traditional shows such as *Follies* (1971) and *Pippin* (1972). To add to the excitement and innovation, Brits Andrew Lloyd Webber and Tim Rice introduced their first rock opera, *Jesus Christ Superstar* (1971), followed by American composer Stephen Schwartz's version on the same Biblical subject, *Godspell* (1971). *Purlie* (1970), *Two Gentlemen of Verona* (1971), *Raisin* (1973), *The Wiz* (1975), and *Ain't Misbehavin'* (1978) featured multiracial and African American casts and themes. *Grease* (1972) set the new record as Broadway's longest-running musical until 1975, when the decade produced another "turning point" show—*A Chorus Line* (1975). This innovative musical had no real set, no special costumes, and a starless ensemble cast of dancers; instead it had a simple book and one of the longest runs on Broadway. These innovations influenced many future productions.

The experimental nature of the decade produced the first all-dance show with no book—*Dancin'* (1978), while the 1975 production of *She-*

nandoah marked the first "country" musical score. After a five-year absence, Stephen Sondheim returned to Broadway in partnership with producer/director Harold Prince to stage *Company* (1970), *Follies* (1971), and *A Little Night Music* (1973). Their innovative "concept" musicals (culture clashes, single life vs. marriage, etc.) reenergized the Broadway musical. Choreographer and director Bob Fosse offered three dance concept musicals: *Pippin* (1972), *Chicago* (1975), and *Dancin'* (1978). Nostalgia for the *Oklahoma*-type book musicals also swept through the American culture during the decade, although most of the revivals were updated with a more contemporary edge. *Applause* (1970), starring Lauren Bacall, was the first hit of the decade. *Purlie* (1970) and *Raisin* (1973), adaptations of previously produced African American dramas, featured a contemporary pop style. The "mega hit" *Annie* (1976) dispelled the belief held by many that the book musical was a dying breed on the Broadway stage.

The end of the decade brought two more hit book musicals: *The Best Little Whorehouse in Texas* (1978) and *They're Playing Our Song* (1979). Sondheim's most adventurous project to date, *Sweeney Todd* (1979), ventured into new emotional territory, featuring a blood-soaked revenge plot set in Victorian London. *Evita* (1979), a hugely successful British import, reaped enormous profits and coined the term "mega musical."

1980–1990

The 1980s were a decade of great variety, ranging from London imports to traditional shows, revivals, and a continuation of rock-style productions. Sondheim, Lloyd Webber, and Claude-Michel Schönberg were the prominent composers of the decade. *42nd Street* (1980), a music comedy based on a classic film, was the first mega hit of the decade, running for 3,486 performances. Several new book musicals, featuring veteran performers as well as a host of newcomers, had successful runs: *Barnum* (1980), *Woman of the Year* (1981), *Nine* (1982), *Little Shop of Horrors* (1982), and *My One and Only* (1983). *Cats* (1982) marked the beginning of the London invasion and revolutionized the focus of the Broadway musical. The revolution, however, had nothing to do with the actual musical, but rather how the show was marketed: the *Cats* logo was added to every object imaginable, becoming one of pop culture's most recognized symbols of the time. The 1983–1984 season was one of the most original on record, with five highly anticipated new musicals reaching the Broadway stage: the underrated *Baby*, *The Tap Dance Kid*, *The Rink*, *Sunday in the Park with George*, and *La Cage Aux Folles*. In 1985, British mega musicals dominated the Broadway scene, introducing *Les Miserables* (1987) and its new "through-sung" musical form, along with the enormously popular *Phantom of the Opera* (1988), a show requiring "legit" singing, but in greatly expanded ranges from the traditional operatic requirements.

In the midst of the "Brit-hits," Sondheim premiered *Into the Woods* (1987), a musical combining revised versions of popular fairy tales. While popular, *Into the Woods* ran for "just" 769 performances, compared to *Les Mis*'s astounding 6,680 performances—and *Phantom of the Opera* is still running today! *Brigadoon* and *My Fair Lady* were revived, though not successfully.

1990–2000

By 1990, attendance at Broadway musicals was at an all-time low, and less than 5 percent of the American public attended theater on a regular basis (Kenrick, 2003). At $60 a ticket, many could simply not afford to visit the Great White Way. The musicals being produced wisely aimed at the core 5 percent audience: *Will Rogers Follies* (1991), *Secret Garden* (1991), *Falsettos* (1992), and *Jelly's Last Jam* (1992). Revivals were important in this decade because investors were reluctant to invest in new productions amid escalating costs. The most successful revivals were *Guys and Dolls* (1992), *Carousel* (1994), *Showboat* (1994), *Crazy for You* (1992), *Kiss of the Spiderwoman* (1993), *Annie Get Your Gun* (1999), and *Kiss Me Kate* (1999). In 1994, the Disney production *Beauty and the Beast* arrived on Times Square, and the impact was significant: the "corporate musical" was born. The presence of Disney in New York was one of the biggest factors in the revival of Times Square, hence Broadway. Once again the area thrived and was deemed safe, and theater benefited. Disney also had success with *The Lion King* (1997) and *Aida* (2000). The British mega musical format was losing its appeal and popularity as evidenced when Andrew Lloyd Webber's *Aspects of Love* (1990) lost over $8 million in spite of a yearlong run.

Rent (1996) was hailed as innovative, as its impact was similar to the 1968 production of *Hair*. The innovation in both those shows pertained to subject matter and vocal production: both the issues and the requirements of the rock singing style are controversial. Rock singing is tough, hard, and driving and often puts immense pressure on the throat muscles. Meanwhile, two revivals of popular Kander and Ebb musicals, *Chicago* (1996) and *Cabaret* (1998), enjoyed long runs. In fact, the production of *Chicago* became the longest-running revival in Broadway history. *Bring in Da' Noise, Bring in Da' Funk* (1996) became the most successful Black musical of the decade. Frank Wildhorn, a new composer, wrote the successful *Jekyll & Hyde* (1997) and *The Scarlet Pimpernel* (1997) and the less successful *Civil War* (1999). The corporate musicals *Titanic* (1997) and *Ragtime* (1998) proved that corporate producers, when coupled with the goal of artistic integrity, could create high-quality work. *Titanic* earned five Tony awards, including Best Musical. *Footloose* (1998) and *Saturday Night Fever* (1999) were popular with audiences, but the critics were unimpressed.

2000–present

Current Broadway productions consist of a mix of revivals (*Man of La Mancha, Gypsy, Hair, Godspell, Annie)* and new productions based on several themes. Movies were well represented with *The Producers* (2001), *The Full Monty* (2001), *Hairspray* (2002), *The Addams Family* (2010), *Sister Act* (2011), and *Spider-man: Turn off the Dark* (2011). Dance themes continued to draw, with *Contact* (2000) and *Movin' Out* (2002). Pop music shows *Mamma Mia* (2001) and *Motown* (2013) spawned the term "jukebox" musical—a musical built around existing pop songs, most often in book form, with more focus on the songs than on the plot. *Aida* (2000), written by Elton John and Tim Rice, was based on the plot of Verdi's opera *Aida*. It featured a pop rock score and enjoyed considerable commercial success.

After the terrorist attacks on September 11, 2001, every theater in New York City went dark for two days, but ten days after the attacks *Urinetown* opened to rave reviews. In 2003, veteran composer-lyricist Stephen Schwartz's sophisticated musical *Wicked* opened and is still running today. In the same year, *Avenue Q*, a low-budget musical featuring puppets, became a sleeper hit, running for 2,534 performances. In 2005, *Monty Python*'s popular *Spamalot* won the Tony for Best Musical in a field richly populated with high-quality productions: *Dirty Rotten Scoun-*

drels, *The Light in the Piazza*, and *The 25th Annual Putnam County Spelling Bee*.

The second half of the decade saw popular music largely replace the show tune. The pop rock style most often dominated the style and sound of the musicals being written and replaced the style of Golden Age composers such as Kern, Berlin, and Rodgers. *Jersey Boys* (2005) was based on the pop music of Frankie Valli and the Four Seasons, becoming the first jukebox musical to win the Tony for Best Musical—to the alarm of some traditionalists. Several very expensive productions did not find success as they had in the past: Andrew Lloyd Webber's *The Woman in White* (2005) and Disney's *Tarzan* (2006) both lost millions of dollars. Even Elton John's score couldn't save *Lestat* (2006), and the failure of Schönberg's *The Pirate Queen* (2006) was further evidence that the mega musical formula was no longer popular. America's Latino population finally came to the forefront with actor-songwriter Lin-Manuel Miranda's successful Off-Broadway production of *In the Heights* (2008). Several successful revivals opened in 2008: *Gypsy*, *South Pacific*, and a bilingual version of *West Side Story*.

In another vein, New York City has always offered popular entertainment during the Christmas season. *A Christmas Carol* ran through the 1990s, and *How the Grinch Stole Christmas* (2006/2007) by Dr. Seuss, Irving Berlin's *White Christmas* (2009/2010), and *Elf* (2010) were all popular and profitable. New productions *The Book of Mormon* (2011), *Once* (2012), and *Newsies* (2012) all continue to enjoy long runs on Broadway. The new productions also represent another important trend in the current decade: as pointed out by expert music theater singing teacher Mary Saunders, what is happening on some of the Broadway stages is bringing together music theater and classical singing. As Saunders points out, "*The Light in the Piazza* is causing this huge shift in the way we look at what is classical style in musical theater singing. The stories are edgier, and the music and use of mix and soprano singing technique is more complicated. What is exciting about this trend is that it brings together contemporary and classical singing in new and thrilling ways" (Mary Saunders, personal communication, April 5, 2006). Saunders and others believe this trend is the wave of the future.

Throughout its long history, the intermingling of styles has always been a dominant characteristic of music theater singing. It is important to understand the chronology of events, and it is equally important to remember that multiple influences, some of them from the distant past, are present in today's music theater. Lastly, these eras provide convenient boundaries for clarification, but most often it is the styles themselves, more than the eras, that combine and influence each other.

BIBLIOGRAPHY

Ciolino, J. (2013). "Biography for Al Jolson." IMDb. Retrieved June 10, 2013, fromhttp://www.imdb.com/name/nm0427231/bio.

Green, S. (1980). *The world of musical comedy*. New York: Da Capo Press, Inc.

Hall, K. S. (2006). Music theater vocal pedagogy and styles: An introductory teaching guide for experienced classical singing teachers. Doctoral Dissertation, Teachers College, Columbia University.

Fandemonium blog. (December 10, 2012). "Broadway Celebrates Best Year Ever." Fandemonium Blog. Retrieved fromhttp://www.vividseats.com/blog/broadway-celebrates-best-year-ever.

———. Musicals101.com. Retrieved April 21, 2013; June 10, 2013; June 13, 2013; June 15, 2013; June 26, 2013; July 7, 2013; July 8, 2013, fromhttp://www.musicals101.com/.

Lubbock, M. (1962). *The complete book of light opera*. New York: Appleton-Century-Crofts.

LoVetri, J. (2013). The necessity of using functional training in the independent studio. *Journal of Singing, 70*(1), 79–86.

Lubbock, M. (1962). American musical theatre: An introduction. In M. Lubbock, *The complete book of light opera* (pp. 753–756). New York: Appleton-Century-Crofts. Retrieved April 21, 2013, and June 6, 2013, fromhttp://www.theatrehistory.com/american/musical030.html.

Roll, C. (2012). *Musical theater singing in the 21st century: Examining the pedagogy of the female belt voice*. Unpublished advanced proposal, Teachers College, Columbia University.

Saunders, Mary. (April 5, 2006). Personal communication.

Shubert Archive. (2002). *The Passing Show, 22*(2). Retrieved fromhttp://www.shubertarchive.org/pdf/passingshows/vol22_2_2002.pdf..

"The Shubert Brothers." (1998). Excerpted from *Encyclopedia of world biography*, 2nd ed. Farmington Hills, Mich.: Gale Research. Retrieved fromhttp://www.pbs.org/wnet/broadway/stars/shubert-brothers/.

Smith, C., and Litton, G. (1950). *Musical comedy in America*. New York: Routledge/Theater Arts Books.

Twain, Mark. "Mark Twain's Illustration of the 'Black Crook.'" *Mariposa Gazette*, volume 12, no. 52 (22 June 1867). Retrieved from http://cdnc.ucr.edu/cgi-bin/cdnc?a=d&d=MG18670622.2.4.

2

SINGING MUSIC THEATER AND VOICE SCIENCE

Scott McCoy

This chapter presents a concise overview of how the voice functions as a biomechanical, acoustic instrument. We will be dealing with elements of anatomy, physiology, acoustics, and resonance. But don't panic: the things you need to know are easily accessible, even if it has been many years since you last set foot in a science or math class!

All musical instruments, including the human voice, have at least four things in common: a *power source*, a *sound source* (vibrator), a *resonator*, and a system for *articulation*. In most cases, the person who plays the instrument provides power by pressing a key, plucking a string, or blowing into a horn. This power is used to set the sound source in motion, which creates vibrations in the air that we perceive as sound. Musical vibrators come in many forms, including strings, reeds, and human lips. The sound produced by the vibrator, however, needs a lot of help before it becomes beautiful music—we might think of it as raw material, like a lump of clay that a potter turns into a vase. Musical instruments use resonance to enhance and strengthen the sound of the vibrator, transforming it into sounds we identify as a piano, trumpet, or guitar. Finally, instruments must have a means of articulation to create the nuanced sounds of music. Let's see how these four elements are used to create the sounds of singing.

PULMONARY SYSTEM: THE POWER SOURCE OF YOUR VOICE

The human voice has a lot in common with a trumpet: both use flaps of tissue as a sound source, both use hollow tubes as resonators, and both rely on the respiratory (pulmonary) system for power. If you stop to think about it, you quickly realize why breathing is so important for singing. First and foremost, it keeps us alive through the exchange of blood gases—oxygen in, carbon dioxide out. But it also serves as the storage depot for the air we use to produce sound. Most singers rarely encounter situations in which these two functions are in conflict, but if you are required to sustain an extremely long phrase, you could find yourself in need of fresh oxygen before your lungs are totally empty.

Misconceptions about breathing for singing are rampant. Fortunately, most are easily dispelled. We must start with a brief foray into the world of physics in the guise of *Boyle's Law*. Some of you no doubt remember this principle: the pressure of a gas within a container changes inversely with changes of volume. If the quantity of a gas is constant and its container is made smaller, pressure rises. But if we make the container bigger, pressure goes down. Boyle's Law explains everything that happens when we breathe, especially when we combine it with another physical law: *nature abhors a vacuum*. If one location has reduced pressure, air flows from an area of higher pressure to equalize the two, and vice versa. So if we can create a zone of reduced air pressure by expanding our lungs, air automatically flows in to restore balance. When air pressure in the lungs is increased, it has no choice but to flow outward.

As we all know, the air we breathe goes in and out of our lungs. Each lung contains millions and millions of tiny air sacs called *alveoli*, where gases are exchanged. The alveoli also function like ultra-miniature versions of the bladder for a bag pipe, storing the air that will be used to set the vocal folds into vibration. To get the air in and out of them, all we need to do is make the lungs larger for inhalation and smaller for exhalation. Always remember this relationship between cause and effect during breathing: we inhale because we make ourselves large; we exhale because we make ourselves smaller. Unfortunately, the lungs are organs, not muscles, and have no ability on their own to accomplish this feat. For this reason, your bodies came from the factory with special muscles designed to enlarge and compress your entire thorax (rib cage), while simultaneously moving your lungs. We can classify these muscles in two main categories: any muscle that has the ability to increase the volume capacity of the thorax serves an *inspiratory* function; any muscle that has the ability to decrease the volume capacity of the thorax serves an *expiratory* function.

Your largest muscle of inspiration is called the *diaphragm* (figure 2.1). This dome-shaped muscle originates from the bottom of your sternum (breastbone) and completely fills the area from that point around your ribs to your spine. It's the second largest muscle in your body, but you probably have no conscious awareness of it or ability to directly control it. When we take a deep breath, the diaphragm contracts and the central portion flattens out and drops downward a couple inches into your abdomen, pressing against all of your internal organs. If you release tension from your abdominal muscles as you inhale, you will feel a gentle bulge in your upper or lower belly or perhaps in your back, resulting from the displacement of your innards by the diaphragm. This is a good thing and can be used to let you know you have taken a good inhalation.

The diaphragm is important, but we must remember that it cannot function in isolation. After you inhale, it relaxes and gently returns to its resting position through an action called *elastic recoil*. This movement, however, is entirely passive and makes no significant contribution to generating the pressure required to sustain phonation. Therefore, it makes no sense at all to try to "sing from your diaphragm"—unless you intend to sing while you inhale, not exhale!

Eleven pairs of muscles assist the diaphragm in its inhalatory efforts, which are called the *external intercostal* muscles (figure 2.2). These muscles start from ribs one through eleven and connect at a slight angle downward to ribs two through twelve. When they contract, the entire thorax moves up and out, somewhat like moving a bucket handle. With the diaphragm and intercostals working together, you are able to increase the capacity of your lungs by about three to six liters, depending on your gender and overall physical stature; thus, we have quite a lot of air available to power our voices.

Eleven additional pairs of muscles are located directly under the external intercostals, which, not surprisingly, are called the *internal intercostals* (figure 2.2). These muscles start from ribs two through twelve and connect upward to ribs one through eleven. When they contract, they induce the opposite action of their external partners: the thorax is made

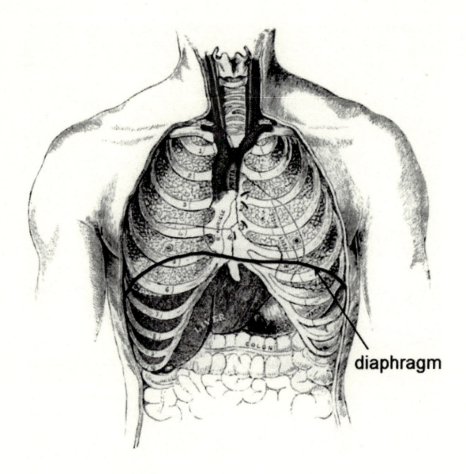

diaphragm

Figure 2.1. Location of Diaphragm

smaller, inducing exhalation. Four additional pairs of expiratory muscles are located in the abdomen, beginning with the *rectus* (figure 2.2). The two rectus abdominis muscles run from your pubic bone to your sternum and are divided into four separate portions, called *bellies* of the muscle (lots of muscles have multiple bellies; it is coincidental that the bellies of the rectus are found in the location we colloquially refer to as our belly). Definition of these bellies results in the so-called ripped abdomen or six-pack of body builders and others who are especially fit.

The largest muscles of the abdomen are called the *external obliques* (figure 2.3), which run at a downward angle from the sides of the rectus, cover the lower portion of the thorax, and extend all the way to the spine.

internal intercostal muscles

external intercostal muscles

rectus abdominis muscles

transverse abdominis muscles (deepest layer)

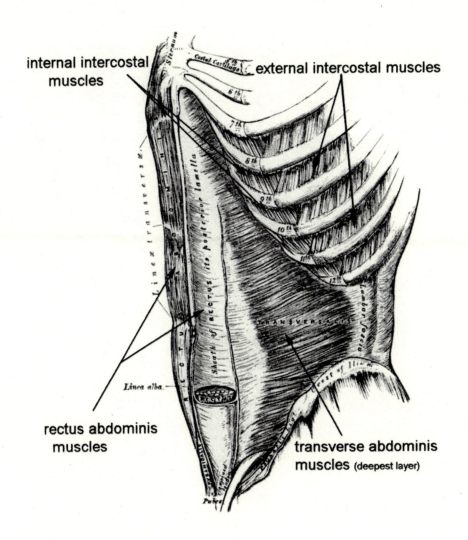

Figure 2.2.   Intercostal and Abdominal Muscles

The *internal obliques* lie immediately below, oriented at an angle that crisscrosses the external muscles. They are slightly smaller, beginning at the bottom of the thorax, rather than extending over it. The deepest muscle layer is the *transverse abdominis* (figure 2.2), which is oriented with fibers that run horizontally. These four muscle pairs completely encase the abdominal region, holding your organs and digestive system in place while simultaneously helping you breathe.

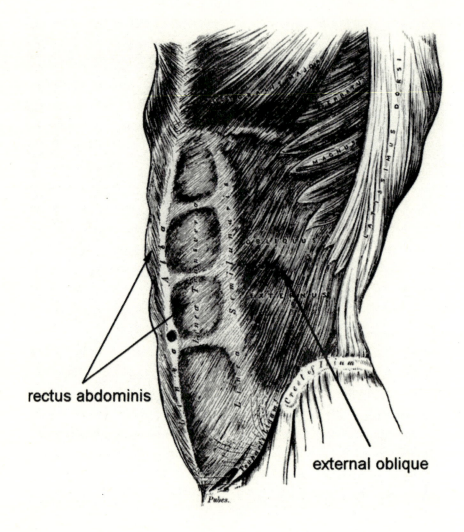

Figure 2.3.   External Oblique and Rectus Abdominis Muscles

Your expiratory muscles are quite large and can produce a great deal of pulmonary, or air, pressure. In fact, they easily can overpower the larynx. Healthy adults generally can generate more than twice the pressure that is required to produce even the loudest sounds; therefore, singers must develop a system for moderating and controlling airflow and breath pressure. This practice goes by many names, including breath support, breath control, and breath management, all of which rely on the principle of *muscular antagonism*. Muscles are said to have an antagonistic relationship when they work in opposing directions, usually pulling on a common point of attachment, for the sake of increasing stability or motor control. You can see a clear example of muscular antagonism in the relationship between your biceps (flexors) and triceps (extensors) when you hold out your arm. In breathing for singing, we activate inspiratory muscles (e.g., diaphragm and external intercostals) during exhalation to help control respiratory pressure and the rate at which air is expelled from the lungs.

One of the things you will notice when watching a variety of singers is that they tend to breathe in many different ways. You might think that voice teachers and scientists, who have been teaching and studying singing for hundreds, if not thousands, of years, would have come to agreement on the best possible breathing technique. But for many reasons, this is not the case. For one, different musical and vocal styles place varying demands on breathing. For another, humans have a huge variety of body types, sizes, and morphologies. A breathing strategy that is successful for a tall, slender woman might be completely ineffective in a short, robust man. Our bodies actually contain a large number of muscles beyond those we've already discussed that are capable of assisting with respiration. For an example, consider your *latissimi dorsi* muscles. These large muscles of the arm enable us to do pull-ups (or pull-downs, depending on which exercise you perform) at the fitness center. But because they wrap around a large portion of the thorax, they also exert an expiratory force. We have at least two dozen such muscles that have secondary respiratory functions, some for exhalation and some for inhalation. When we consider all these possibilities, it is no surprise at all that there are many ways to breathe that can produce beautiful singing. Just remember to practice some muscular antagonism—maintaining a degree of inhalation posture during exhalation—and you should do well.

LARYNX: THE VIBRATOR OF YOUR VOICE

The larynx, sometimes known as the voice box or Adam's apple, is a complex physiologic structure made of cartilage, muscle, and tissue. Biologically, it serves as a sphincter valve, closing off the airway to prevent foreign objects from entering the lungs. When firmly closed, it also is used to increase abdominal pressure to assist with lifting heavy objects, childbirth, and defecation. But if we gently close this valve while we exhale, tissue in the larynx begins to vibrate and produce the sounds that become speech and singing.

The human larynx is a remarkably small instrument, typically ranging from the size of a pecan to a walnut for women and men, respectively. Sound is produced at a location called the *glottis*, which is formed by two flaps of tissue called the *vocal folds* (aka vocal cords). In women, the glottis is about the size of a dime; in men, it can approach the diameter of a quarter. The two folds are always attached together at their front point, but open in the shape of the letter V during normal breathing, an action called *abduction*. To phonate, we must close the V while we exhale, an action called *adduction* (just like the machines you use at the fitness center to exercise your thigh and chest muscles).

Phonation only is possible because of the unique multilayer structure of the vocal folds (figure 2.4). The core of each fold is formed by muscle, which is surrounded by a layer of gelatinous material called the *lamina propria*. The *vocal ligament* also runs through the lamina propria, which helps to prevent injury by limiting how far the folds can be stretched for high pitches. A thin, hairless epithelial layer that is constantly kept moist with mucus secreted by the throat, larynx, and trachea surrounds all of this. During phonation, the outer layer of the fold glides independently over the inner layer in a wavelike motion, without which phonation is impossible.

We can use a simple demonstration to better understand the independence of the inner and outer portions of the folds. Explore the palm of your hand with your other index finger. Note that the skin is attached quite firmly to the flesh beneath it. If you poke at your palm, that flesh acts as padding, protecting the underlying bone. Now explore the back of your hand. You will observe that the skin is attached quite loosely—you easily can move it around with your finger. And if you poke at the back of your hand, it is likely to hurt; there is very little padding between the skin and your bones. Your vocal folds combine the best attributes of both sides of your hand. They provide sufficient padding to help reduce impact stress, while permitting the outer layer to slip like the skin on the back of your hand, enabling phonation to occur. When you are sick with laryngitis and lose your voice (a condition called *aphonia*), inflammation in the vocal folds couples the layers of the folds tightly together. The outer layer

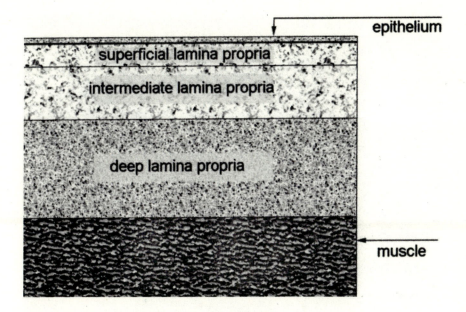

Figure 2.4. Layered Structure of the Vocal Fold

no longer can move independently over the inner and phonation becomes difficult or impossible.

The vocal folds are located within the five cartilaginous structures of the larynx (figure 2.5). The largest is called the *thyroid cartilage*, which is shaped like a small shield. The thyroid connects to the *cricoid* cartilage below it, which is shaped like a signet ring—broad in the back and narrow in the front. Two cartilages that are shaped like squashed pyramids sit atop the cricoid, called the *arytenoids*. Each vocal fold runs from the thyroid cartilage in front to one of the arytenoids at the back. Finally, the *epiglottis* is located at the top of the larynx, flipping backward each time we swallow to prevent food and liquid from entering our lungs. Muscles connect between the various cartilages to open and close the glottis, and to lengthen and shorten the vocal folds for ascending and descending pitch, respectively. Because they sometimes are used to identify vocal function, it is a good idea to know the names of the muscles that control the length of the folds. We've already mentioned that a muscle forms the core of each fold. Because it runs between the thyroid cartilage and an arytenoid, it is named the *thyroarytenoid* muscle (formerly known as the *vocalis* muscle). When the thyroarytenoid, or TA, muscle contracts, the

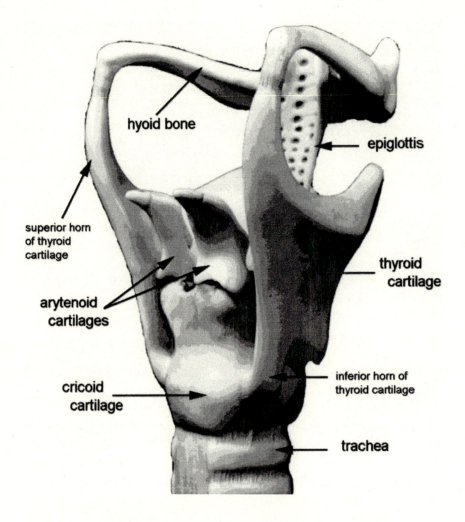

Figure 2.5. **Cartilages of the Larynx, Viewed at an Angle from the Back**

fold is shortened and pitch goes down. The folds are elongated through the action of the *cricothyroid*, or CT, muscles, which run from the thyroid to cricoid cartilage.

Vocal color (timbre) is created by the combined effects of the sound produced by the vocal folds and the resonance provided by the vocal tract. While these elements can never be completely separated, it is useful to consider the two primary modes of vocal fold vibration and their resulting sound qualities. The main differences are related to the relative thickness of the folds and their cross-sectional shape (figure 2.6). The first option depends on short, thick folds that come together with nearly square-shaped edges. Vibration in this configuration is given a variety of names, including *Mode 1*, *Thyroarytenoid* (TA) *dominant, chest mode,* or *modal voice*. The alternate configuration uses longer, thinner folds that only make contact at their upper margins. Common names include *Mode 2, Cricothyroid* (CT) *dominant, falsetto mode,* or *loft voice*. Singers vary the vibrational mode of the folds according to the quality of sound they wish to produce.

Before we move on to a discussion of resonance, we must consider the quality of the sound that is produced by the larynx. At the level of the glottis, we create a sound not unlike the annoying buzz of a duck call. That buzz, however, contains all the raw material we need to create speech and singing. Vocal or glottal sound is considered to be *complex*, meaning it consists of many simultaneously sounding frequencies (pitches). The lowest frequency within any tone is called the *fundamental*, which corresponds to its named pitch in the musical scale. Orchestras tune to a pitch called A-440, which means it has a frequency of 440 vibrations per second, or 440 *Hertz* (abbreviated Hz). Additional frequencies are included above the fundamental, which are called *overtones*. Overtones in the glottal sound are quieter than the fundamental. In voices, the overtones usually are whole number multiples of the fundamental, creating a pattern called the *harmonic series* (e.g., 100Hz, 200Hz, 300Hz, 400Hz, 500Hz, etc. or G2, G3, C4, G4, B4) (figure 2.7).

Singers who choose to make coarse or rough sounds as might be appropriate for rock or blues, often add overtones that are *inharmonic*, or not part of the standard numerical sequence. Inharmonic overtones also are common in singers with damaged or pathological voices.

Glottis configuration
in mode 1 (chest voice)

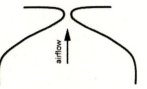
Glottis configuration
in mode 2 (falsetto)

Figure 2.6.   Primary Modes of Vocal Fold Vibration

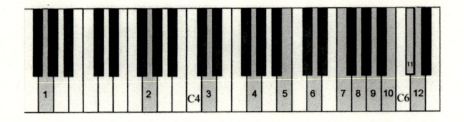

Figure 2.7.   Natural Harmonic Series, Beginning at G2

Under most circumstances, we are completely unaware of the presence of overtones—they simply contribute to the overall timbre of a voice. In some vocal styles, however, harmonics become a dominant feature. This is especially true in *throat singing* or *overtone singing*, as is found in places like Tuva. Throat singers tune their vocal tracts so precisely that single harmonics are highlighted within the harmonic spectrum as a separate, whistle-like tone. These singers sustain a low-pitched drone and then create a melody by moving from tone to tone within the natural harmonic series. You can learn to do this too. Sustain a comfortable pitch in your range and slowly morph between the vowels /ee/ and /oo/. If you listen carefully, you will hear individual harmonics pop out of your sound.

The mode of vocal fold vibration has a strong impact on the overtones that are produced. In mode 1, high frequency harmonics are relatively strong; in mode 2, they are much weaker. As a result, mode 1 tends to yield a much brighter, brassier sound.

VOCAL TRACT: YOUR SOURCE OF RESONANCE

Resonance typically is defined as the amplification and enhancement (or enrichment) of musical sound through *supplemental vibration*. What does this really mean? In layman's terms, we could say that resonance makes instruments louder and more beautiful by reinforcing the original vibrations of the sound source. This enhancement occurs in two primary ways, which are known as forced and free resonance. Any object that is physically connected to a vibrator can serve as a forced resonator. For a piano, the resonator is the soundboard (on the underside of a grand or on the back of an upright); the vibrations of the strings are transmitted directly to the soundboard through a structure known as the bridge, which also is found on violins and guitars. Forced resonance also plays a role in voice production. Place your hand on your chest and say *ah* at a low pitch. You almost certainly felt the vibrations of forced resonance. In singing, this might best be considered your *private* resonance; you can feel it and it might impact your self-perception of sound, but nobody else can hear it. To understand why this is true, imagine what a violin would sound like if it were encased in a thick layer of foam rubber. The vibrations of the string would be damped out, muting the instrument. Your skin, muscles, and other tissues do the same thing to the vibrations of your vocal folds.

By contrast, free resonance occurs when sound travels through a hollow space, such as the inside of a trumpet, an organ pipe, or your vocal tract, which consists of the pharynx (throat), oral cavity (mouth), and nasal cavity. As sound travels through these regions, a complex pattern of echoes is created; every time sound encounters a change in the shape of the vocal tract, some of its energy is reflected backward, much like an echo in a canyon. If these echoes arrive back at the glottis at the precise moment a new pulse of sound is created, the two elements synchronize, resulting in a significant increase in intensity. All of this happens very quickly—remember that sound is traveling through your vocal tract at more than seven hundred miles per hour.

Whenever this synchronization of the vocal tract and sound source occurs, we say that the system is *in resonance*. The phenomenon occurs at specific frequencies (pitches), which can be varied by changing the position of the tongue, lips, jaw, palate, and larynx. These resonant frequencies, or areas in which strong amplification occurs, are called *formants*. Formants provide the specific amplification that changes the raw, buzzing sound produced by your vocal folds into speech and singing. The vocal tract is capable of producing many formants, which are labeled sequentially by ascending pitch. The first two, F_1 and F_2, are used to create vowels; higher formants contribute to the overall timbre and individual characteristics of a voice. In some singers, especially those who train to sing in opera, formants three through five are clustered together to form a super formant, eponymously called the *singer's formant*, which creates a ringing sound and enables a voice to be heard in a large theater without electronic amplification.

Formants are vitally important in singing, but they can be a bit intimidating to understand. An analogy that works really well for me is to think of formants like the wind. You cannot see the wind, but you know it is present when you see leaves rustling in a tree or feel a breeze on your face. Formants work in the same manner. They are completely invisible and directly inaudible. But just as we see the rustling leaf, we can hear, and perhaps even feel, the action of formants through how they change our sound. Try a little experiment. Sing an ascending scale beginning at B-flat$_3$, sustaining the vowel /ee/. As you approach the D-natural or E-flat of the scale, you likely will feel (and hear) that your sound becomes a bit stronger and easier to produce. This occurs because the scale tone and formant are on the same pitch, providing additional amplification. If you change to an /oo/ vowel, you will feel the same thing at about the same place in the scale. If you sing to an /oh/ or /eh/ and continue up the scale, you'll feel a bloom in the sound somewhere around C$_5$ (an octave above middle-C). /ah/ is likely to come into its best focus at about G$_5$.

To remember the approximate pitches of the first formants for the main vowels, ee-eh-ah-oh-oo, just think of a C-Major triad in first inversion, open position, starting at E$_4$: ee = E$_4$, eh = C$_5$, ah = G$_5$, oh = C$_5$, and oo = E$_4$ (figure 2.8). If your music theory isn't strong, you could use the mnemonic "**e**very **c**hild **g**ets **c**andy **e**agerly." These pitches might vary by as much as a minor third higher and lower, but no farther: once a formant changes by more than that interval, the vowel that is produced *must* change.

Formants have absolutely no preference for what they amplify—they are indiscriminate lovers, just as happy to bond with the first harmonic as

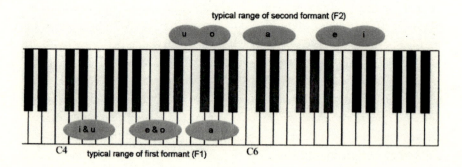

Figure 2.8. Typical Range of First and Second Formants for Primary Vowels

the fifth. When men or women sing low pitches, there almost always will be at least one harmonic that comes close enough to a formant to produce a clear vowel sound. The same is not true for women with high voices, especially sopranos, who routinely must sing pitches that have a fundamental frequency *higher* than the first formant of many vowels. Imagine what happens if she must sing the phrase "and I'll leave you forever," with the word "leave" set on a very high, climactic note. The audience won't be able to tell if she is singing *leave* or *love* forever; the two will sound identical. This happens because the formant that is required to identify the vowel /ee/ is too far below the pitch being sung. Even if she tries to sing *leave*, the sound that comes out of her mouth will be heard as some variation of /ah/.

Fortunately, this kind of mismatch between formants and musical pitches rarely causes problems for anyone but opera singers, choir sopranos, and perhaps ingénues in classic music theater shows. Almost everyone else generally sings low enough in their respective voice ranges to produce easily identifiable vowels.

Second formants also can be important, but more so for opera singers than everyone else. They are much higher in pitch, tracking the pattern oo = E_5, oh = G_5, ah = D_6, eh = B_6, ee = D_7 (you can use the mnemonic "**e**very **g**ood **d**ad **b**uys **d**iapers" to remember these pitches) (figure 2.8). Because they can extend so high, into the top octave of the piano keyboard for /ee/, they interact primarily with higher tones in the natural harmonic series. Unless you are striving to produce the loudest unamplified sound possible, you probably never need to worry about the second formant; it will steadfastly do its job of helping to produce vowel sounds without any conscious thought or manipulation on your part.

If you are interested in discovering more about resonance and how it impacts your voice, you might want to install a spectrum analyzer on your computer. Free (or inexpensive) programs are readily available for download over the Internet that will work with either a PC or Mac computer. You don't need any specialized hardware—if you can use Skype or FaceTime, you already have everything you need. Once you've installed something, simply start playing with it. Experiment with your voice to see exactly how the analysis signal changes when you change the way your voice sounds. You'll be able to see how harmonics change in intensity as they interact with your formants. If you sing with vibrato, you'll see how consistently you produce your variations in pitch and amplitude.

You'll even be able to see if your tone is excessively nasal for the kind of singing you want to do. Other programs are available that will help you to improve your intonation (how well you sing in tune) or to enhance your basic musicianship skills. Technology truly has advanced sufficiently to help us sing more beautifully.

MOUTH, LIPS, AND TONGUE: YOUR ARTICULATORS

The articulatory life of a singer is not easy, especially when compared to the demands placed on other musicians. Like a pianist or brass player, we must be able to produce the entire spectrum of musical articulation, including dynamic levels from hushed pianissimos to thunderous fortes, short notes, long notes, accents, crescendos, diminuendos, and so on. We produce most of these articulations the same way instrumentalists do, which is by varying our power supply. But singers have another layer of articulation that makes everything much more complicated; we must produce these musical gestures while simultaneously singing words.

As we learned in our brief examination of formants, altering the resonance characteristics of the vocal tract creates the vowel sounds of language. We do this by changing the position of our tongue, jaw, lips, and sometimes palate. Slowly say the vowel pattern ee-eh-ah-oh-oo. Can you feel how your tongue moves in your mouth? For /ee/, it is high in the front and low in the back, but it takes the opposite position for /oo/. Now slowly say the word *Tuesday*, noting all the places your tongue comes into contact with your teeth and palate, and how it changes shape as you produce the vowels and diphthongs. There is a lot going on in there—no wonder it takes so long for babies to learn to speak!

Our articulatory anatomy is extraordinarily complex, in large part because our bodies use the same passageway for food, water, air, and sound. As a result, our tongue, larynx, throat, jaw, and palate are all interconnected with common physical and neurologic points of attachment. Our anatomical Union Station in this regard is a small structure called the *hyoid bone*. The hyoid is one of only three bones in your entire body that do not connect to other bones via a joint (the other two are your *patellae*, or kneecaps). This little bone is suspended below your jaw, freely floating up and down every time you swallow. It is a busy place, serving as the upper suspension point for the larynx, the connection for the root of the tongue, and the primary location of the muscles that open your mouth by dropping your jaw.

Good singing—in any genre—requires a high degree of independence in all these articulatory structures. Unfortunately, nature conspires against us to make this difficult to accomplish. From the time we were born, our bodies have relied on a reflex reaction to elevate the palate and raise the larynx each time we swallow. This action becomes habitual: palate goes up, larynx also lifts. But depending on the style of music we are singing, we might need to keep the larynx down while the palate goes up (opera and classical), or palate down with the larynx up (country and bluegrass). As we all know, habits can be very hard to change, which is one of the reasons that it can take a lot of study and practice to become an excellent singer. Understanding your body's natural reflexive habits can make some of this work a bit easier.

There is one more significant pitfall to the close proximity of all these articulators: tension in one area is easily passed along to another. If your jaw muscles are too tight while you sing, that hyperactivity will likely be transferred to the larynx and tongue—remember, they all are interconnected through the hyoid bone. It can be tricky to determine the primary offender in this kind of chain reaction of tension. A tight tongue could just as easily be making your jaw stiff, or an elevated, rigid larynx could make both tongue and jaw suffer.

Neurology complicates matters even further. You have sixteen muscles in your tongue, fourteen in your larynx, twenty-two in your throat and palate, and another sixteen that control your jaw. Many of these are very small and lie directly adjacent to each other, and you often are required to contract one quite strongly while its next-door neighbor must remain totally relaxed. Our brains need to develop laser-like control, sending signals at the right moment with the right intensity to the precise spot where they are needed. When we first start singing, these brain signals come more like a blast from a shotgun, spreading the neurologic impulse over a broad area to multiple muscles, not all of which are the intended target. Again, with practice and training we learn to refine our control, enabling us to use only those muscles that will help, while disengaging those that would get in the way of our best singing.

CONCLUSION

This brief chapter has only scratched the surface of the huge field of voice science. To learn more, you might visit the websites of the National Association of Teachers of Singing, the Voice Foundation, or the National Center for Voice and Speech. You can easily locate the appropriate addresses through any Internet search engine. Remember: knowledge is power. Occasionally, people are afraid that if they know more about the science of how they sing, they will become so analytical that all spontaneity is lost or they will become paralyzed by too much information and thought. In my forty-plus years as a singer and teacher, I've never encountered somebody who actually suffered this fate. To the contrary, the more we know, the easier—and more joyful—singing becomes.

3

VOCAL HEALTH AND THE MUSIC THEATER VOCAL ATHLETE

Wendy DeLeo LeBorgne

GENERAL PHYSICAL WELL-BEING

All singers, regardless of genre, should consider themselves as "vocal athletes." The physical, emotional, and performance demands required for optimal output require that, as an artist and vocal athlete, you train and maintain your instrument like an athlete trains for an athletic event. With increased vocal and performance demands, it is unlikely that a vocal athlete will have an entire performing career completely injury free. This may not be the fault of the singer as many injuries occur due to circumstances beyond the singer's control, such as singing through an illness or being on a new medication seemingly unrelated to the voice.

Vocal injury has often been considered taboo to talk about in the performing world as it has been considered to be the result of faulty technique or poor vocal habits. In actuality, the majority of vocal injuries presenting in the elite performing population tend to be overuse and/or acute injury. From a clinical perspective over the past seventeen years, younger, less experienced singers with fewer years of training (who tend to be quite talented) generally are the ones who present with issues related to technique or phonotrauma (nodules, edema, contact ulcers), while more mature singers with professional performing careers tend to present with acute injuries (hemorrhage), overuse and misuse injuries (muscle tension dysphonia, edema, GERD), or injuries following an illness. There are no current studies documenting use and training in correlation to laryngeal pathologies. However, there are studies which document that somewhere between 35 percent and 100 percent of professional vocal athletes have abnormal vocal fold findings on stroboscopic evaluation (Korovin & LeBorgne, 2009; Phyland, Oates, & Greenwood, 1999; Hoffman-Ruddy, Lehman, Crandell, Ingram, & Sapienza, 2001; LeBorgne, Donahue, Brehm, & Weinrich, 2012; Evans, Evans, Carvajal, & Perry, 1996; Koufman, Radomski, Joharji, Russell, & Pillsbury, 1996; Heman-Ackah, Dean, & Sataloff, 2002; Lundy, Casiano, Sullivan, Roy, Xue, & Evans, 1999; Tepe, Deutsch, Sampson, Lawless, Reilly, & Sataloff, 2002). Many times these "abnormalities" are in singers who have no vocal complaints or symptoms of vocal problems. From a performance perspective, uniqueness in vocal quality often gets hired and perhaps a slight aberration in the way a given larynx functions may become quite marketable. Regardless of what the vocal folds may look like, the most integral part of performance is that the singer must maintain agility, flexibility, stamina, power, and inherent beauty (genre appropriate) for their current level of performance taking into account physical, vocal, and emotional demands.

Unlike sports medicine and the exercise physiology literature where much is known about the types and nature of given sports injuries, there is no common parallel for the vocal athlete model (Yang, Tibbetts, Covassin, Cheng, Nayar, & Heiden, 2012). However, because the vocal athlete utilizes the body systems of alignment, respiration, phonation, and resonance with some similarities to physical athletes, a parallel protocol for vocal wellness may be implemented/considered for vocal athletes to maximize injury prevention knowledge for both the singer and teacher. This chapter aims to provide information on vocal wellness and injury prevention for the vocal athlete.

CONSIDERATIONS FOR WHOLE BODY WELLNESS

Nutrition

You have no doubt heard the saying "You are what you eat." Eating is a social and psychological event. For many people, food associations and eating have an emotional basis resulting in either overeating or being malnourished. Eating disorders and body image issues in performers may have major implications and consequences for the performer on both ends of the spectrum (obesity and anorexia). Singers should be encouraged to reprogram the brain and body to consider food as fuel. You want to use high-octane gas in your engine, as pouring water in your car's gas tank won't get you very far. Eating a poor diet or a diet that lacks appropriate nutritional value will have negative physical and vocal effects on the singer. Effects of poor dietary choices for the vocal athlete may result in physical and vocal effects ranging from fatigue to life-threatening disease over the course of a lifetime. Encouraging and engaging in healthy eating habits from a young age will potentially prevent long-term negative effects from poor nutritional choices. It is beyond the scope of this chapter to provide a complete overview of all the dietary guidelines for children, adolescents, adults, and mature adults; however, a listing of additional references to help guide your food and beverage choices for making good nutritional choices can be found online at:

Dietary Guidelines for Americans: http://www.health.gov/
    dietaryguidelines/
Nutrition.gov Guidelines for Tweens and Teens: http://www.nutrition.
    gov/life-stages/adolescents/tweens-and-teens
Fruits and Veggies Matter: http://www.fruitsandveggiesmorematters.
    org/myplate-and-what-is-a-serving-of-fruits-and-vegetables

Hydration

"Sing wet, pee pale." This phrase was echoed in the studio of Dr. Van Lawrence regarding how his students would know if they were well-enough hydrated. Generally, this rule of pale urine during your waking hours is a good indicator that you are well hydrated. Medications, vitamins, and certain foods may alter urine color despite adequate hydration. Due to the varying levels of physical and vocal activity of many performers, in order to maintain adequate oral hydration, the use of a hydration calculator based on activity level may be a better choice. These hydration calculators are easily accessible online and take into account the amount and level of activity the performer engages in on a daily basis. In a recent study of the vocal habits of music theater performers, one of the findings indicated a significantly underhydrated group of performers (Donahue, LeBorgne, Brehm, & Weinrich, in review.

Laryngeal and pharyngeal dryness as well as "thick, sticky, mucus" are often complaints of singers. Combating these concerns and maintaining an adequate viscosity of mucus for performance has resulted in some research. As a reminder of laryngeal and swallowing anatomy, nothing that is swallowed (or gargled) goes over or touches the vocal folds directly (or one would choke). Therefore, nothing that you eat or drink ever touches the vocal folds and in order to adequately hydrate the mucus membranes of the vocal folds, one must consume enough fluids for the body to produce thin mucus. Therefore, any "vocal" effects from swallowed products are limited to potential pharyngeal and oral changes, not the vocal folds themselves.

The effects of systemic hydration are well documented in the literature. There is evidence to suggest that adequate hydration will provide some protection of the laryngeal mucosal membranes when they are placed under increased collision forces as well as reduce the amount of effort (phonation threshold pressure) to produce voice (Leydon, Sivasankar, Falciglia, Atkins, & Fisher, 2009; Leydon, Wroblewski, Eichorn, & Sivasankar, 2010; Sivasankar & Leydon, 2010; Yiu & Chan, 2003). This is important for a singer because it means that with adequate hydration and consistency of mucus, the effort to produce voice is less and your vocal folds are better protected from injury. Imagine the friction and heat produced when two dry hands rub together and then what happens if you put lotion on your hands. The mechanisms in the larynx to provide appropriate mucus production are not fully understood, but there is enough evidence at this time to support oral hydration as a vital component of every singer's vocal health regime to maintain appropriate mucosal viscosity.

Although very rare, overhydration (hyperhidrosis) can result in dehydration and even illness or death. An overindulgence of fluids essentially makes the kidneys work "overtime" and flushes too much water out of the body. This excessive fluid loss in a rapid manner can be detrimental to the body.

In addition to drinking water to systemically monitor hydration, there are many nonregulated products on the market for performers that lay claim to improving the laryngeal environment (e.g., Entertainer's Secret, Throat Coat Tea, Greathers Pastilles, Slippery Elm, etc.). Although there may be little detriment in using these products, quantitative research documenting change in laryngeal mucosa is sparse (Brinckmann, Sigwart, &

vanHouten Taylor, 2003; Roy, Tanner, Gray, Blomgren, & Fisher, 2003). One study suggests that the use of Throat Coat when compared to a placebo treatment for pharyngitis did show a significant difference in decreasing the perception of sore throat. Another study compared the use of Entertainer's Secret to two other nebulized agents and its effect on phonation threshold pressure (PTP). There was no positive benefit in decreasing PTP with Entertainer's Secret.

Many singers use personal steam inhalers and/or room humidification to supplement oral hydration and aid in combating laryngeal dryness. There are several considerations for singers who choose to use external means of adding moisture to the air they breathe. Personal steam inhalers are portable and can often be used backstage or in the hotel room for the traveling performer. Typically, water is placed in the steamer and the face is placed over the steam for inhalation. Because the mucus membranes of the larynx are composed of a saltwater solution, one study looked at the use of nebulized saline in comparison to plain water and its potential effects on effort or ease to sound production in classically trained sopranos (Tanner, Roy, Merrill, Muntz, Houtz, Sauder, Elstad, & Wright-Costa, 2010). Data suggested that perceived effort to produce voice was less in the saline group than the plain water group. This indicated that the singers who used the saltwater solution reported less effort to sing after breathing in the salt water than singers who used plain water. It was hypothesized by the researchers that because the body's mucus is not plain water (rather it is a salt water—think about your tears), that when you use plain water for steam inhalation, it may actually draw the salt from your own saliva, resulting in a dehydrating effect.

In addition to personal steamers, other options for air humidification come in varying sizes of humidifiers from room size to whole house humidifiers. When choosing between a warm air and cool mist humidifier, considerations include both personal preference and needs. One of the primary reasons warm mist humidifiers are not recommended for young children is due to the risk of burns from the heating element. Both the warm mist and cool air humidifiers act similarly in adding moisture to the environmental air. External air humidification may be beneficial and provide a level of comfort for many singers. Regular cleaning of the humidifier is vital to prevent bacteria and mold buildup. Also, depending on the hardness of the water, it is important to avoid mineral buildup on the device and distilled water may be recommended for some humidifiers.

For traveling performers who often stay in hotels, fly on airplanes, or are generally exposed to other dry air environments, there are products on the market designed to help minimize drying effects. One such device is called a Humidflyer, which is a facemask (http://www.humidiflyer.com/) designed with a filter to recycle the moisture of your own breath and replenish moisture on each breath cycle.

For dry nasal passages or to clear sinuses, many singers use neti pots. Many singers use this homeopathic flushing of the nasal passages regularly. When utilized properly research supports the use of a neti pot as a part of allergy relief and chronic rhinosinusitis control, sometimes in combination with medical management (Brown & Grahm, 2004; Dunn, Dion, & McMains, 2013). Conversely, long-term use of nasal irrigation (without taking intermittent breaks from daily use) may result in washing out the "good" mucus of the nasal passages, which naturally help to rid the nose of infections. A study presented at the American College of Allergy, Asthma & Immunology (ACAAI) 2009 Annual Scientific Meeting reported that when a group of individuals who were using twice-daily nasal irrigation for one year discontinued using it, they had an increase in acute rhinosinusitis (Nsouli, 2009).

TEA, HONEY, AND GARGLE TO KEEP THE THROAT HEALTHY

Regarding the use of general teas (which many singers combine with honey or lemon), there is likely no harm in the use of decaffeinated tea (caffeine may cause systemic dryness). The warmth of the tea may provide a soothing sensation to the pharynx and the act of swallowing can be relaxing for the muscles of the throat. Honey has shown promising as an effective cough suppressant in the pediatric population (Shadkam, Mozaffari-Khosravi, & Mozayan, 2010). The dose of honey given to the children in the study was two teaspoons. Gargling with salt or apple cider vinegar and water are also popular home remedies for many singers with the uses being from soothing the throat to curing reflux. Gargling plain water has been shown to be efficacious in reducing the risk of contracting upper respiratory infections (Satomura, Kitamura, Kawamura, Shimbo, Watanabe, Kamei, Takana, & Tamakoshi, 2005). I suggest that when you gargle, you only "bubble" the water with air and avoid engaging the vocal folds in sound production. Salt water as a gargle has long been touted as a sore throat remedy and can be traced back to 2700 BC in China for treating gum disease (http://health.howstuffworks.com/wellness/oral-care/products/saltwater-as-mouthwash.htm). The science behind a salt-water rinse for everything from oral hygiene to sore throat is that salt (sodium chloride) may act as a natural analgesic (pain killer) and may also kill bacteria. Similar to not enough salt in the water drawing the salt out of the tissue in the steam inhalation, if you oversaturate the water solution with excess salt and gargle it, it may act to draw water out of the oral mucosa, thus reducing inflammation.

Another popular home remedy reported by singers is the use of apple cider vinegar to help with everything from acid reflux to sore throats. Dating back to 3300 BC, apple cider vinegar was reported as a medicinal remedy, and it became popular in the 1970s as a weight loss diet cocktail. Popular media reports apple cider vinegar can improve conditions from acne and arthritis to nosebleeds and varicose veins (http://www. healthline.com/natstandardcontent/apple-cider-vinegar). Specific efficacy data regarding the beneficial nature of apple cider vinegar for the purpose of sore throat, pharyngeal inflammation, and/or reflux have not been reported in the literature at this time. Of the peer-reviewed studies found in the literature, one discussed possible esophageal erosion and inconsistency of actual product in tablet form (Hill, Woodruff, Foote, & Barreto-Alcoba, 2005). Therefore, at this time, strong evidence supporting the use of apple cider vinegar is not published.

MEDICATIONS AND THE VOICE

Medications (over the counter, prescription, and herbal) may have resultant drying effects on the body and often the laryngeal mucosa. General classes of drugs with potential drying effects include: antidepressants, antihypertensives, diuretics, ADD/ADHD medications, some oral acne medications, hormones, allergy drugs, and vitamin C in high doses. The National Center for Voice and Speech (NCVS) provides a listing of some common medications with potential voice side effects including laryngeal dryness. This listing does not take into account all medications so singers should always ask their pharmacist of the potential side effects of a given medication. Due to the significant number of drugs on the market, it is safe to say that most pharmacists will not be acutely aware of "vocal side effects," but if dryness is listed as a potential side effect of the drug, you may assume that all body systems could be affected. Under no circumstances should you stop taking a prescribed medication without consulting your physician first. As every person has a different body chemistry and reaction to medication, just because a medication lists dryness as a potential side effect, it does not necessarily mean you will experience that side effect. Conversely, if you begin a new medication and notice physical or vocal changes that are unexpected, you should consult with your physician. Ultimately, the goal of medical management for any condition is to achieve the most benefits with the least side effects. A list of possible resources for singers regarding prescription drugs and herbs is:

- http://www.fda.gov/OHRMS/DOCKETS/98FR/06D-0480-GLD0001.PDF
- http://nccam.nih.gov/health/herbsataglance.htm
- http://www.nlm.nih.gov/medlineplus/druginfo/herb_All.html
- http://www.ncvs.org

In contrast to medications that tend to dry, there are medications formulated to increase saliva production or alter the viscosity of mucus. Medically, these drugs are often used to treat patients who have had a loss of saliva production due to surgery or radiation. Mucalytic agents are used to thin secretions as needed. As a singer if you feel that you need to use a mucalytic agent on a consistent basis, it may be worth considering getting to the root of the laryngeal dryness symptom and seeking a professional opinion from an otolaryngologist.

PHYSICAL EXERCISE

Vocal athletes, like other physical athletes, should consider how and what they do to maintain both cardiovascular fitness and muscular strength. In today's performance culture, it is rare that a performer stands still and sings, unless in a recital or choral setting. The range of physical activity can vary from light movement to high-intensity choreography with acrobatics. As performers are being required to increase their onstage physical activity level from the operatic stage to the pop star arena, overall physical fitness is imperative to avoid compromise in the vocal system. Breathlessness will result in compensation by the larynx that is now attempting to regulate the air. Compensatory vocal behaviors over time may result in a change in vocal performance. The health benefits of both cardiovascular training and strength training are well documented in the literature for physical athletes, but relatively rare for vocal performers.

MENTAL WELLNESS

Vocal performers must maintain a mental focus during performance and a mental toughness during auditioning and training. Rarely during vocal performance training programs is this important aspect of performance addressed, and it is often left to the individual performer to develop their own strategy or coping mechanism. Yet, many performers are on anti-anxiety or antidepressant drugs (which may be the direct result of performance-related issues). If the sports world is again used as a parallel for mental toughness, there are no elite-level athletes (and many junior-level athletes) who don't utilize the services of a performance/sports psychologist to maximize focus and performance. I recommend that performers consider the potential benefits of a performance psychologist to help maximize vocal performance. Several references that may be of interest to a singer include: Joanna Cazden's *Visualization for Singers* and Shirlee Emmons & Alma Thomas's *Power Performance for Singers: Transcending the Barriers*.

Unlike instrumentalists, whose performance is dependent on accurate playing of an external musical instrument, the singer's instrument is uniquely intact and subject to the emotional confines of the brain and body in which it is housed. Musical performance anxiety (MPA) can be career threatening for all musicians, but perhaps the vocal athlete is more severely impacted (Spahn, Echternach, Zander, Voltmer, & Richter, 2010). The majority of literature on MPA is dedicated to instrumentalists, but the basis of definition, performance effects, and treatment options can be considered for vocal athletes (Anderson, 2011; Arneson, 2010; Brantigan, Brantigan, & Joseph, 1982; Brugues, 2011; Chanel, 1992; Corby, n.d.; Drinkwater & Klopper, 2010; Fehm & Schmidt, 2006; Fredrikson & Gunnarsson, 1992; Gates, Saegert, Wilson, Johnson, Shepherd, & Hearne, 1985; Gates & Montalbo, 1987; Kenny, Davis, & Oates, 2004;

Khalsa, Shorter, Cope, Wyshak, & Sklar, 2009; Lazarus & Abramovitz, 2004; Markovska-Simoska, McGinnis, & Milling, 2005; Pop-Jordanova & Georgiev, 2008; Nagel, 2010; Neftel, Adler, Käppeli, Rossi, Dolder, Käser, Bruggesser, & Vorkauf, 1982; Powell, 2004; Schneider & Chesky, 2011; Spahn et al., 2010; Studer, Danuser, Hildebrandt, Arial, & Gomez, 2011; Studer, Gomez, Hildebrandt, Arial, & Danuser, 2011; Taborsky, 2007; van Kemenade, van Son, & van Heesch, 1995; Walker & Nordin-Bates, 2010; Wesner, Noyes, & Davis, 1990).

Fear is a natural reaction to a stressful situation, and there is a fine line between emotional excitation and perceived threat (real or imagined). The job of a performer is to convey to an audience through vocal production, physical gestures, and facial expression a most heightened state of emotion. Otherwise, why would audience members pay top dollar to sit for two or three hours for a mundane experience? Not only is there the emotional conveyance of the performance, but also the internal turmoil often experienced by a singer in preparation for elite performance. It is well documented in the literature that even the most elite performers have experienced debilitating performance anxiety. MPA is defined on a continuum with anxiety levels ranging from low to high and has been reported to comprise four distinct components: affect, cognition, behavior, and physiology (Spahn et al., 2010). Affect comprises feelings (e.g., doom, panic, anxiety); affected cognition will result in altered levels of concentration; while the behavior component results in postural shifts, quivering, and trembling; and finally physiologically the body's ANS system will activate, resulting in the "fight or flight" response. In recent years, researchers have been able to define two distinct neurological pathways for MPA. The first pathway happens quickly and without conscious input (ANS), resulting in the same fear stimulus as if a person were put into an emergent, life-threatening situation. In those situations, the brain releases adrenaline resulting in physical changes of: increased heart rate, increased respiration, shaking, pale skin, dilated pupils, slowed digestion, bladder relaxation, dry mouth, and dry eyes, all of which severely affect vocal performance. The second pathway that has been identified results in a conscious identification of the fear/threat and a much slower physiologic response. With the second neuromotor response, the performer has a chance to recognize the fear, process how to deal with the fear, and respond accordingly.

Treatment modalities to address MPA include psycho-behavioral therapy (including biofeedback) and drug therapies. Elite physical performance athletes have been shown to benefit from visualization techniques and psychological readiness training, yet within the performing arts community, stage fright may be considered a weakness or character flaw precluding readiness for professional performance. On the contrary, vocal athletes, like physical athletes, should mentally prepare themselves for optimal competition (auditions) and performance. Learning to convey emotion without eliciting an internal emotional response by the vocal athlete may take the skill of an experienced psychologist to help change ingrained neural pathways. Ultimately, control and understanding of MPA will enhance performance and prepare the vocal athlete for the most intense performance demands without vocal compromise.

VOCAL WELLNESS: INJURY PREVENTION

In order to prevent vocal injury and understand vocal wellness in the singer, general knowledge of common causes of voice disorders is imperative. One common cause of voice disorders is vocally abusive behaviors or misuse of the voice, including phonotraumatic behaviors such as yelling, screaming, loud talking, talking over noise, throat clearing, coughing, harsh sneezing, and boisterous laughing. Chronic or less than optimal vocal properties such as poor breathing techniques, inappropriate phonatory habits during conversational speech (glottal fry, hard glottal attacks), inapt pitch, loudness, rate of speech, and/or hyperfunctional laryngeal area muscle tone may also negatively impact vocal function. Medically related etiologies, which also have the potential to impact vocal function, range from untreated chronic allergies and sinusitis to endocrine dysfunction and hormonal imbalance. Direct trauma, such as a blow to the neck or the risk of vocal fold damage during intubation, can impact optimal performance in vocal athletes depending on the nature and extent of the trauma. Finally, external irritants ranging from cigarette smoke to reflux directly impact the laryngeal mucosa and ultimately can lead to laryngeal pathology. Vocal hygiene education and compliance may be one of the primary essential components for maintaining the voice throughout a career (Behrman, Rutledge, Hembree, & Sheridan, 2008). This section will provide the singer with information on prevention of vocal injury. However, just like a professional sports athlete, it is unlikely that a professional vocal athlete will go through an entire career without some compromise in vocal function. This may be a common upper respiratory infection that creates vocal fold swelling for a short time or it may be a "vocal accident" that is career threatening. Regardless, the knowledge of how to take care of your voice is essential for any vocal athlete.

Train Like an Athlete for Vocal Longevity

Performers seek instant gratification in performance sometimes at the cost of gradual vocal building for a lifetime of healthy singing. Historically, vocal pedagogues required their students to perform vocalise exclusively for up to two years before beginning any song literature. Singers gradually built their voice by ingraining appropriate muscle memory and neuromotor patterns through development of aesthetically pleasing tones, onsets, breath management, and support. There was an intensive master-apprentice relationship and rigorous vocal guidelines to maintain a place within a given studio. Time off was taken if a vocal injury ensued, or careers potentially were ended and students were asked to leave a given singing studio if their voice was unable to withstand the rigors of training. Training vocal athletes today has evolved and appears driven to create a "product" quickly, perhaps at the expense of the longevity of the singer. Pop stars emerging well before puberty are doing international concert tours, yet many young artist programs in the classical arena do not consider singers for their programs until they are in their mid to late twenties.

Each vocal genre presents with different standards and vocal demands. Therefore, the amount and degree of vocal training is varied. Some would argue that performing extensively without adequate vocal training and development is ill advised; yet singers today are thrust onto the stage at very young ages. Dancers, instrumentalists, and physical athletes all spend many hours per day developing muscle strength, muscle memory, and proper technique for their craft. The more advanced the artist or athlete, generally the more specific the training protocol becomes. Consideration of training vocal athletes in this same fashion is recommended. One would generally not begin a young, inexperienced singer without previous vocal training on a Wagner aria. Similarly, in nonclassical vocal music, there are easy, moderate, and difficult pieces to consider pending level of vocal development and training.

Basic pedagogical training of alignment, breathing, voice production, and resonance are essential building blocks for development of good voice production. Muscle memory and development of appropriate muscle patterns happens slowly over time with appropriate repetitive practice. Doing too much, too soon for any athlete (physical or vocal) will result in an increased risk for injury. When the singer is being asked to do "vocal gymnastics," they must be sure to have a solid basis of strength and stamina in the appropriate muscle groups to perform consistently with minimal risk of injury.

Vocal Fitness Program

One generally does not get out of bed first thing in the morning and try to do a split. Yet many singers go directly into a practice session or audition without proper warm-up. Think of your larynx like your knee, made up of cartilages, ligaments, and muscles. Vocal health is dependent upon appropriate warm-ups (to get things moving), drills for technique, and then cool-downs (at the end of your day). Consider vocal warm-ups a "gentle stretch." Depending on the needs of the singer, warm-ups should include physical stretching; postural alignment self checks; breathing exercises to promote rib cage, abdominal, and back expansion; vocal stretches (glides up to stretch the vocal folds and glides down to contract the vocal folds); articulatory stretches (yawning, facial stretches); and mental warm-ups (to provide focus for the task at hand). Vocalises, in my opinion, are designed as exercises to go beyond warm-ups and prepare the body and voice for the technical and vocal challenges of the music they sing. They are varied and address the technical level and genre of the singer to maximize performance and vocal growth. Cool-downs are a part of most athletes' workouts. However, singers often do not use cool-downs (physical, mental, and vocal) at the end of a performance. A recent study looked specifically at the benefits of vocal cool-downs in singers and found that singers who used a vocal cool-down had decreased effort to produce voice the next day (Gottliebson, 2011).

Systemic hydration as a means to keep the vocal folds adequately lubricated for the amount of impact and friction that they will undergo has been previously discussed in this chapter. Compliance with adequate oral hydration recommendations is important and subsequently the minimization of agents that could potentially dry the membranes (e.g., caffeine, medications, dry air). The body produces approximately two quarts of mucus per day. If not adequately hydrated, the mucus tends to be thick and sticky. Poor hydration is similar to not putting enough oil in the car engine. Frankly, if the gears do not work as well, there is increased friction and heat, and the engine is not efficient.

Speak Well, Sing Well

Optimize the speaking voice utilizing ideal frequency range, breath, intensity, rate, and resonance. Singers generally are vocally enthusiastic individuals who talk a lot and often talk loudly. During typical conversation, the average fundamental speaking frequency (times per second the vocal folds are impacting) for a male varies from 100 to 150 Hz and 180 to 230 Hz for women. Because of the delicate structure of the vocal folds and the importance of the layered microstructure vibrating efficiently and effectively to produce voice, vocal behaviors or outside factors that compromise the integrity of the vibration patterns of the vocal folds may be considered phonotrauma.

Phonotraumatic behaviors can include yelling, screaming, loud talking, harsh sneezing, and harsh laughing. Elimination of phonotraumatic behaviors is essential for good vocal health. The louder one speaks, the farther apart the vocal folds move from midline, the harder they impact, and the longer they stay closed. A tangible example would be to take your hands, move them only six inches apart and clap as hard and as loudly as you can for ten seconds. Now, move your hands two feet apart and clap as hard, loudly, and quickly as possible for ten seconds. The farther apart your hands are, the more air you move, the louder the clap, and the skin on the hands becomes red and ultimately swollen (if you do it long enough and hard enough). This is what happens to the vocal folds with repeated impact at increased vocal intensities. The vocal folds are approximately 17 mm in length and vibrate at 220 times per second on A3, 440 times on A4, 880 times on A5, and more than 1,000 times per second when singing a high C. That is a lot of impact for little muscles. Consider this fact when singing loudly or in a high tessitura for prolonged periods of time. It becomes easy to see why women are more prone then men to laryngeal impact injuries due to the frequency range of the voice alone.

In addition to the amount of cycles per second the vocal folds are impacting, singers need to be aware of their vocal intensity (volume).

Check the volume of the speaking and singing voice and for conversational speech and consider using a distance of three to five feet as a gauge for how loud you need to be in general conversation (about an arm's length distance). Cell phones and speaking on a Bluetooth device in a car generally result in louder than conversational vocal intensity, and singers are advised to minimize unnecessary use of these devices.

Singers should be encouraged to take "vocal naps" during their day. A vocal nap would be a short period of time (five minutes to an hour) of complete silence. Although the vocal folds are rarely completely still (because they move when you swallow and breathe), a vocal nap minimizes impact and vibration for a short window of time. A physical nap can also be refreshing for the singer mentally and physically.

Avoid Environmental Irritants: Alcohol, Smoking, and Drugs

Arming singers with information on the actual effects of environmental irritants so that they can make informed choices on engaging in exposure to these potential toxins is essential. The glamour that continues to be associated with smoking, drinking, and drugs can be tempered with the deaths of popular stars such as Amy Winehouse and Cory Monteith who engaged in life-ending choices. There is extensive documentation about the long-term effects of toxic and carcinogenic substances, but here are a few key facts to consider when choosing whether to partake.

Alcohol, although it does not go over the vocal folds directly, does have a systemic drying effect. Due to the acidity in alcohol, it may increase the likelihood of reflux, resulting in hoarseness and other laryngeal pathologies. Consuming alcohol generally decreases one's inhibitions, and therefore you are more likely to sing and do things that you would not typically do under the influence of alcohol.

Beyond the carcinogens in nicotine and tobacco, the heat at which a cigarette burns is well above the boiling temperature of water (water boils at 212 degrees Fahrenheit; a cigarette burns at over 1,400 degrees Fahrenheit). No one would consider pouring a pot of boiling water on their hand, and yet the burning temperature for a cigarette results in significant heat over the oral mucosa and vocal folds. The heat alone can create deterioration in the lining, resulting in polypoid degeneration. Obviously, cigarette smoking has been well documented as a cause for laryngeal cancer.

Marijuana and other street drugs are not only addictive, but can cause permanent mucosal lining changes depending on the drug used and the method of delivery. If you or one of your singer colleagues is experiencing a drug or alcohol problem, provide them with information and support on getting appropriate counseling and help.

SMART PRACTICE STRATEGIES FOR SKILL DEVELOPMENT AND VOICE CONSERVATION

Daily practice and drills for skill acquisition is an important part of any singer's training. However, overpracticing or inefficient practicing may be detrimental to the voice. Consider practice sessions of athletes: they may practice four to eight hours per day broken into one- to two-hour training sessions with a period of rest and recovery in between sessions. Although we cannot parallel the sports model without adequate evidence in the vocal athlete, the premise of short, intense, focused practice sessions is logical for the singer. Similar to physical exercise, it is suggested that practice sessions do not have to be all "singing." Rather, structuring sessions so that one-third of the session is spent on warm-up; one-third on vocalise, text work, rhythms, character development, and so on; and one-third on repertoire will allow the singer to function in a more efficient vocal manner. Building the amount of time per practice session, increasing duration by five minutes per week, and building from sixty to ninety minutes may be effective (e.g., week one: twenty minutes, three times per day; week two: twenty-five minutes, three times per day, etc.).

Vary the "vocal workout" during your week. For example, if you do the same physical exercise in the same way day after day with the same intensity and pattern, you will likely experience repetitive strain type injuries. However, cross-training or varying the type and level of exercise aids in injury prevention. So when planning your practice sessions for a given week (or rehearsal process for a given role), consider varying your vocal intensity, tessitura, and exercises to maximize your training sessions, building stamina, muscle memory, and skill acquisition. For example, one day you may spend more time on learning rhythms and translation and the next day you spend thirty minutes performing coloratura exercises to prepare for a specific role. Take one day a week off from vocal training and give your voice a break. This does not mean complete vocal rest (although some singers find this beneficial), but rather a day without singing and with limited talking.

Practice Your Mental Focus

Mental wellness and stress management are equally as important as vocal training for vocal athletes. Addressing any mental health issues is paramount to developing the vocal artist. This may include anything from daily mental exercises/meditation/focus to overcoming performance anxiety to more serious mental health issues/illness. Every person can benefit from improved focus and mental acuity.

SPECIFIC VOCAL WELLNESS CONCERNS FOR THE MUSIC THEATER SINGER

Music theater performers must sing, dance, and act with equal strength to be competitive in the professional arena. Vocally, the industry demands that music theater singers produce believable and stylistically appropriate sounds from a legit classical to raucous heavy metal scream and everything in between. Vocal gymnastics are performed while completely out of breath (from dancing, hanging from the ceiling, roller skating, etc.) on sets with moving parts and uneven surfaces, in costumes that compromise posture and breathing for eight shows a week. This presents a unique demand on the music theater singer with respect to maintaining a healthy body and instrument. In addition to all of the above recommendations, here are some specific recommendations for vocal health in the music theater performer.

Physical Fitness

The commercial look of contemporary music theater performers is often a fit, flexible actor. To achieve this chiseled physique requires cardiovascular training, weight lifting/resistance training, diet modification, and often intensive dance training. For roles that require significant dancing and singing, it is highly advisable for the music theater performer to consider cardiovascular interval training. Cardiovascular interval training requires a singer to go from an easy heart rate, to a moderate heart rate, to a maximal heart rate and then drop back down to the easy heart rate for a specified time interval. Doing this type of training improves cardiovascular fitness and quick recovery to a normal heart rate.

Pending the physical demands of a given role, strength training and core strength training provide the singer a means to avoid laryngeal compensation. Consider roles that physically demand that a performer sing from a static physical position requiring core strength for stability. If the core strength of that performer is not adequate, over the course of time, the performer will begin to rely on stability somewhere else in the body (larynx, neck muscles, etc.) to produce the desired sound. Ultimately, compensation may lead to negative vocal and physical patterns. Diet and exercise for music theater performers to support their physical and vocal demands are imperative for continued success.

Healthy Belting

Belting is a requirement of music theater performers and has historically gotten a bad reputation for being potentially harmful to the voice and leading to laryngeal pathology. If classical singing is analogous to an Olympic athlete, belting is analogous to an X-Game athlete. Both can be performed at an elite level with training, practice, and talent, but may have inherent vocal risk due to the intensity and frequency of repeated performance. Research on whether healthy belting can be performed eight shows a week is sparse. However, indications of abnormal laryngeal findings in incoming collegiate-level vocal athletes who belt are no greater than that of classical singers (LeBorgne et al., 2012; Elias, Sataloff, Rosen, Heuer, & Spiegel, 1997; Evans et al., 1996; Evans, Evans, & Carvajal, 1998, Heman-Ackah et al., 2002; Hoffman-Ruddy et al., 2001; Lundy et al., 1999).

Music theater performers must belt to be competitive in the professional arena. Even at the high school and junior-high school levels, belting is required for theater productions. Therefore, singers are going to belt to meet the demands of the industry, and without instruction on how to do it properly (utilizing appropriate breath pressure, vocal fold vibration, and resonators to enhance and amplify the sound, in conjunction with microphone techniques) performers may be at higher risk of injury. The aim of this section is not pedagogical, but many vocal pedagogues question if the belt voice can be taught effectively and safely as both the

American Academy of Teachers of Singing and the Voice Foundation gently caution singers and teachers about the possible detrimental effects of belting in the past (Colla, 1989; Estill, 1988; Howell, 1991; Shapiro, 1987; Sullivan, 1989; Timberlake, 1986; Miles & Hollien, 1990). Belting seemingly pushed the vocal mechanism to its physiological limits in a different way than ingénues of the past, and many questioned whether or not it would damage the vocal mechanism. Unlike the classical voice, belting has been considered emotionally edgy and verging on the brink of sounding out of control. It is this unique quality that so many singers have attempted to emulate in the past sixty years. There is no denying that the belt voice has established itself as a vocal quality that is desired and hired in the professional arena and as such demands attention to healthy production.

Healthy production of the belt voice based on literature regarding its physiologic and acoustic properties (as well as personal experience— more than twenty years of belting training) indicate that music theater performers must (1) speak well and be able to appropriately project the speaking voice, (2) utilize breathing strategies that support the intensity of sound production, (3) warm up appropriately before singing at physiologic vocal extremes, (4) perform belt literature that is age, technically, and emotionally appropriate for the level of the singer, (5) allow for periods of cross-training (e.g., use all parts of the voice) during training and performance of intensive belting, and (6) learn to use the resonators as natural amplifiers as well as using microphones and amplification to boost acoustic power (LeBorgne, 2001).

A brief word on amplification for the music theater performer as a means to maximize vocal health: amplification does not preclude good singing technique. Rather, amplification in music theater venues (from amateur productions to professional shows) allows the singer to produce voice in an efficient manner while the sound engineer is effectively able to mix, amplify, and add effects to the voice. All professional music theater performances (and many amateur productions) use amplification, and a good sound engineer is a vital component to vocal preservation in this performance arena. Emulating the recorded singing of electronically enhanced and boosted voices at the same intensity level in a practice room or live performance situation is ill advised and can occasionally be an impetus for phonotrauma in the music theater singer.

Not everything a singer does is "vocally healthy," but cross-training the instrument (which can mean singing in both high and low registers with varying intensities and resonance options) is likely a vital component to minimizing vocal injury. Ultimately, the singer must learn to provide the most output with the least "cost" to the system. Taking care of your physical instrument through daily physical exercise, adequate nutrition and hydration, and maintaining focused attention on performance will provide a necessary basis for vocal health during performance. Small doses of high-intensity singing (or speaking) will limit impact stress on the vocal folds. Finally, attention to the mind, body, and voice will provide the singer with an awareness when something is wrong. This awareness and knowledge of when to rest or seek help will promote vocal well-being for you throughout your career.

BIBLIOGRAPHY

Anderson, L. (2011). Myself or someone like me: A review of the literature on the psychological well-being of child actors. *Medical Problems of Performing Artists, 36*(3), 146–49.

Behrman, A., Rutledge, J., Hembree, A., & Sheridan, S. (2008). Vocal hygiene education, voice production therapy, and the role of patient adherence: A treatment effectiveness study in women with phonotrauma. *Journal of Speech, Language, and Hearing Research, 51,* 350–66.

Brantigan, C., Brantigan, T., & Joseph N. (1982). Effect of beta blockade and beta stimulation on stage fright. *American Journal of Medicine, 72*(1), 88–94.

Brinckmann, J., Sigwart, H., & vanHouten Taylor, L. (2003). Safety and efficacy of a traditional herbal medicine (Throat Coat) in symptomatic temporary relief of pain in patients with acute pharyngitis: A multicenter, prospective, randomized, double-blinded, placebo- controlled study. *Journal of Alternative and Complementary Medicine, 9*(2), 285–98. Retrieved from http://www.ncbi.nlm.nih.gov/pubmed/?term=Throat+coat+tea.

Brown, C. & Grahm, S. (2004). Nasal irrigations: Good or bad? *Current Opinion in Otolaryngology, Head and Neck Surgery, 12*(1), 9–13.

Brugués, A. (2011a). Music performance anxiety—Part 1. A review of treatment options. *Medical Problems of Performing Artists, 26*(2), 102–5.

Brugués, A. (2011b). Music performance anxiety—Part 2. A review of treatment options. *Medical Problems of Performing Artists, 26*(3), 164–71.

Chanel, P. (1992). Performance anxiety. *American Journal of Psychiatry, 149*(2), 278–79.

Colla, R. (1989). To belt correctly or not to belt that should be the question. *The NATS Journal,* January/February 39–40, 51.

Donahue, E., LeBorgne, W., Brehm, S., & Weinrich, B. (2013). Reported vocal habits of first-year undergraduate musical theater majors in a preprofessional training program: A 10-year retrospective study. *Journal of Voice (In Press)*.

Drinkwater, E., & Klopper, C. (2010). Quantifying the physical demands of a musical performance and their effects on performance quality. *Medical Problems of Performing Artists, 25*(2), 66–71.

Dunn, J., Dion, G., & McMains, K. (2013). Efficacy of nasal symptom relief. *Current Opinion in Otolaryngology—Head and Neck Surgery, 21*(3), 248–51.

Elias, M. E., Sataloff, R. T., Rosen, D. C., Heuer, R. J., & Spiegel, J. R. (1997). Normal strobovideolaryngoscopy: Variability in healthy singers. *Journal of Voice*, *11*(1), 104–7.

Evans, R. W., Evans, R. I., & Carvajal, S. (1998). Survey of injuries among west end performers. *Occupational and Environmental Medicine*, *55*, 585–93.

Evans, R. W., Evans, R.I., Carvajal, S., & Perry, S. (1996). A survey of injuries among Broadway performers. *American Journal of Public Health*, *86*, 77.

Fredrikson, M., & Gunnarsson, R. (1992). Psychobiology of stage fright: The effect of public performance on neuroendocrine, cardiovascular and subjective reactions. *Biology Psychology*, *33*(1), 51–61.

Gates, G., Saegert, J., Wilson, N., Johnson, L., Shepherd, A., & Hearne, E. (1985). Effect of beta blockade on singing performance. *Annals of Otology, Rhinology, and Laryngology*, *94*(6).

Gottliebson, R.O. (2011). The efficacy of cool-down exercises in the practice regimen of elite singers. Dissertation, University of Cincinnati.

Heman-Ackah, Y., Dean, C., & Sataloff, R. T. (2002). Strobovideolaryngoscopic findings in singing teachers. *Journal of Voice*, *16*(1), 81–86.

Hill, L., Woodruff, L., Foote, J., & Barreto-Alcoba, M. (2005). Esophageal injury by apple cider vinegar tablets and subsequent evaluation of products. *Journal of the American Dietetics Association*, *105*(7), 1141–44.

Hoffman-Ruddy, B., Lehman, J., Crandell, C., Ingram, D., & Sapienza, C. (2001). Laryngostroboscopic, acoustic, and environmental characteristics of high-risk vocal performers. *Journal of Voice*, *15*(4), 543–52.

Kenny, D., Davis, P., & Oates, J. (2004). Music performance anxiety and occupational stress amongst opera chorus artists and their relationship with state and trait anxiety and perfectionism. *Journal of Anxiety Disorders*, *18*(6), 757–77. (Pt 1), 570–74.

Koufman, J. A., Radomski, T. A., Joharji, G. M., Russell, G. B., & Pillsbury, D. C. (1996). Laryngeal biomechanics of the singing voice. *Otolaryngology—Head and Neck Surgery*, *115*, 527–37.

Korovin, G., & LeBorgne, W. (2009). A longitudinal examination of potential vocal injury in musical theater performers. The Voice Foundation's 36th Annual Symposium: Care of the Professional Voice, June 3–7, 2009, Philadelphia, PA.

Lazarus, A., & Abramovitz, A. (2004). A multimodal behavioral approach to performance anxiety. *Journal of Clinical Psychology*, *60*(8), 831–40.

LeBorgne, W. (2001). Defining the belt voice: Perceptual judgments and objective measures. Dissertation, University of Cincinnati.

LeBorgne, W., Donahue, E., Brehm, S., & Weinrich, B. (2012). Prevalence of vocal pathology in incoming freshman musical theatre majors: A 10-year retrospective study, Fall Voice Conference, October 4–6, 2012, New York.

Leydon, C., Sivasankar, M., Falciglia, D., Atkins, C., & Fisher, K. (2009). Vocal fold surface hydration: A review. *Journal of Voice*, *23*(6): 658–65.

Leydon, C., Wroblewski, M., Eichorn, N., & Sivasankar, M. (2010). A meta-analysis of outcomes of hydration intervention on phonation threshold pressure. *Journal of Voice*, *24*(6), 637–43.

Lundy, D., Casiano, R., Sullivan, P., Roy, S., Xue, J., & Evans, J. (1999). Incidence of abnormal laryngeal findings in asymptomatic singing students. *Otolaryngology—Head and Neck Surgery*, *121*, 69–77.

Nagel, J. (2010). Treatment of music performance anxiety via psychological approaches: A review of selected CBT and psychodynamic literature. *Medical Problems of Performing Artists*, *25*(4), 141–48.

Nsouli, T. Long-term use of nasal saline irrigation: Harmful or helpful? American College of Allergy, Asthma & Immunology (ACAAI) 2009 Annual Scientific Meeting, Abstract 32, November 8, 2009.

Phyland, D. J., Oates, J., & Greenwood, K. (1999). Self-reported voice problems among three groups of professional singers. *Journal of Voice*, *13*, 602–11.

Powell, D. (2004). Treating individuals with debilitating performance anxiety: An introduction. *Journal of Clinical Psychology*, *60*(8), 801–8.

Roy, N., Tanner, K., Gray, S., Blomgren, M., & Fisher, K. (2003). An evaluation of the effects of three laryngeal lubricants on phonation threshold pressure (PTP). *Journal of Voice, 17*(3), 331–42. Retrieved from http://www.ncbi.nlm.nih.gov/pubmed/?term= Entertainer%E2%80%99s+Secret.

Satomura, K., Kitamura, T., Kawamura, T., Shimbo, T., Watanabe, M., Kamei, M., Takana, Y., & Tamakoshi, A. (2005). Prevention of upper respiratory tract infections by gargling: A randomized trial. *American Journal of Preventative Medicine, 29*(4), 302–7.

Shadkam, M., Mozaffari-Khosravi, H., & Mozayan, M. (July 2010). A comparison of the effect of honey, dextromethorphan, and diphenhydramine on nightly cough and sleep quality in children and their parents. *Journal of Alternative and Complementary Medicine, 16*(7), 787–93.

Shapiro, J. (1987). I want to sing like Madonna-how come I have to sing Vaccaii? *Jazz Educators Journal*, October/November, 15–16, 45.

Sivasankar, M., & Leydon, C. (2010). The role of hydration in vocal fold physiology. *Current Opinion in Otolaryngology & Head and Neck Surgery, 18*(3), 171–75.

Spahn, C., Echternach, M., Zander, M., Voltmer, E., & Richter, B. (2010). Music performance anxiety in opera singers. *Logopedica Phoniatrica Vocology, 35*(4), 175–82.

Studer, R., Gomez, P., Hildebrandt, H., Arial, M., & Danuser, B. (2011). Stage fright: Its experience as a problem and coping with it. *International Archives of Occupational Environmental Health, 84*(7), 761–71.

Sullivan, J. (1989). How to teach the belt/pop voice. *Journal of Research in Singing and Applied Vocal Pedagogy, 13*(1), 41–56.

Tanner, K., Roy, N., Merrill, R., Muntz, F., Houtz, D., Sauder, C., Elstad, M., & Wright-Costa, J. (2010). Nebulized isotonic saline versus water following a laryngeal desiccation challenge in classically trained sopranos. *Journal of Speech Language and Hearing Research, 53*(6), 1555–66.

Tepe, E. S., Deutsch, E. S., Sampson, Q., Lawless, S., Reilly, J. S., & Sataloff, R. T. (2002). A pilot survey of vocal health in young singers. *Journal of Voice , 16*, 244–47.

Timberlake, C. (1986). The 'pop' singer and the voice teacher (From the American Academy of Teachers of Singing). *The NATS Journal*, September/October, 21, 31.

Yang, J., Tibbetts, A., Covassin, T., Cheng, G., Nayar, S., & Heiden, E. (2012). Epidemiology of overuse and acute injuries among competitive collegiate athletes. *Journal of Athletic Training, 47*(2), 198–204.

Yiu, E., & Chan, R. (2003). Effect of hydration and vocal rest on the vocal fatigue in amateur karaoke singers. *Journal of Voice, 17*, 216–27.

4

MUSIC THEATER VOCAL PEDAGOGY

In this chapter, we take a look at the basics in mastering one's voice in music theater singing: breathing, posture, registers, tone quality adjustment/resonance, range, and dynamics. These are the techniques you need to develop in order to become a healthy and successful music theater singer. Exercises for developing these techniques are located at the NATS website, http://www.nats.org. Click on the "resources" link and follow the instructions.

OVERVIEW OF MUSIC THEATER SINGING HISTORY

The information that follows applies mostly to what is commonly called female mix/belt singing. The dictionary defines the word *belt*, a verb, "to hit very hard." It can be argued that belt singing sounds as though it is being hit very hard. Belt singing has an intensity and "on edge" energy that is unmistakable. A "belter" is a singer that sings in the belt quality. Belt becomes an adjective when describing the quality: a "belt song" (LoVetri, 2012).

In many cultures worldwide belt singing has been the norm for centuries. The American music theater female belt voice was first heard on the Broadway stage at the beginning of the nineteenth century to enable the unamplified, speech-like female voice to be audible in the middle and lower ranges. These vocal changes were caused by a shift in the theatrical and musical demands found in the music theater compositions of that time (Green, 1980; Roll, 2012).

European operetta heavily influenced the music theater productions of the late 1800s and early 1900s (Roll, 2012). For a host of reasons, often the European operetta imports had songs inserted by other composers, resulting in a jumbled collection of music and story line. Composer Jerome Kern was often asked to compose songs to insert into another composer's operetta. Determined to change the current practice, Kern incorporated mix/belt vocal changes with his groundbreaking musical *Showboat*. Even though *Showboat* contained characteristics of the operetta style, the music was "representative of the characters who sing them" (Green, 1980, 52; Roll, 2012). Kern wanted the characters in *Showboat* to sing like they spoke. This requirement meant singers had to develop new vocal strategies to create a more speech-like sound, particularly in the speaking voice range C_4–C_5.

Ethel Merman is often credited with creating the first Broadway belt sound (Roll, 2012). "From its inception on Broadway, the belt sound has been linked with the theatrical need to communicate a stronger emotion with heightened sound and understandable text" (Roll, 2012, 5). The belt sound began to appear with increasing regularity on the Broadway stage, and by the 1980s and 1990s, it was the dominant female sound. In addition, when older shows were revived during this time (and today as well), often a more "legit" role was sung with a mix/belt vocal production.

Another turning point in terms of vocal production occurred in the 1960s with the introduction of the pop/rock musical form. The 1968 production of *Hair* did not use any of the traditional singing sounds. It was based on the new rock genre reflecting the social changes occurring in America. "Its commercial and critical success opened the door to a new era of musical theater composition that is still occurring and evolving over fifty years later: the rock/pop musical" (Roll, 2012, 6–7). *Hair* also used authentic electric rock instruments and instrumentation that meant the singing voices had to be amplified. The use of amplification soon became standard on the music theater stage. Today, the pop/rock style and sound is the dominant form used by music theater composers; the composers also want singers to sing in the pop/rock style (Roll, 2012). These compositional demands of the pop/rock style have created the need for females and males to sing in the belt range at higher pitch levels (beyond the C_4–C_5 range).

While males also use mix/belt vocal production in music theater, the vocal changes men make are accomplished in a higher part of the vocal range, at the secondo *passaggio*, an Italian term referring to a vocal register pivotal point, where the registration event of moving from "chest" to "head" register occurs. The high male passaggio, or secondo passaggio, is located at the approximate pitch range C_4–E_4, depending on the size and type of voice. To date, little to no voice science research has been conducted on the male belt voice. In the male voice, most believe a narrowing of the vocal tract that causes the vocal sound to brighten produces male belting. To contrast, in classical male singing, the pitches in the passaggio range are darkened, modified, or "covered."

In music theater singing, understanding and communication of the text is the most important aspect of vocal production. Mix/belt singing is considered an extension of the speaking voice. Women use the mix/belt voice production in a lower part of their voice, the C_4–C_5 range. In the past ten years, because of the vocal demands of the new repertoire (mostly pop/rock), females have started taking their mix/belt singing up to E_5 and beyond. Interestingly, oftentimes the rock musicals of the 1960s addressed the topical political and social issues of the day. One of the social changes under way during the 1960s was the equal rights movement and shifting gender roles. The 1960s musicals mirrored those changes by creating female and male characters that sing in approximately the same vocal range.

BRIEF OVERVIEW OF THE VOCAL SYSTEM

The power source (breath), the vibrator (vocal folds), and the resonator (vocal tract) are the three parts of the body that interact together to form the vocal system. The breath, vocal folds, and vocal tract interact together to create the singing voice. The breath from the lungs sets the vocal folds in motion and the vocal tract creates the color, timbre, and resonance of your voice. Singing requires more oxygen than speech as well as a longer and controlled exhale than speaking (Doscher, 1994; Roll, 2012). When you inhale a singing breath, the rib cage expands and the diaphragm relaxes and lowers, which creates space in the abdomen allowing the lungs to fill with air. The exhale is slow and controlled while maintaining rib expansion. The slow, controlled exhale creates either air flow (low and middle range) or air pressure (high range) to maintain appropriate vocal fold vibration (Doscher, 1994).

For a more detailed explanation, refer to chapter 2 by Dr. Scott McCoy.

STYLISTIC AND PEDAGOGICAL CHARACTERISTICS OF MUSIC THEATER SINGING

The lists below summarize the pedagogical and stylistic characteristics most commonly found in music theater female singing, followed by explanations and definitions of the characteristics (LoVetri, 2004).

Stylistic Characteristics

- Physical "typing" is the norm
- Songs and roles are learned as needed, not beforehand
- Females sing in the soprano and alto range
- Men sing in the tenor and baritone range
- Acting must be excellent
- Singing is text driven, enunciation of the text dominates singing
- Voices are electronically amplified
- Not necessary to read music
- Sing eight shows a week for the run of a show
- Styles change frequently
- Many untrained singers work without difficulty
- Songs are transposed as needed
- Dance skills needed
- Musical values vary

Pedagogical Characteristics

- Pharyngeal region is similar to speech
- Larynx is in the mid or high position
- Mouth shape is horizontal
- In females most vowels have a "brighter" color that is created by the use of more chest register (other names for this type of vocal fold

vibration are mode 1, thyroarytenoid [TA] dominant, model voice) and/or by altering the resonance to a brighter, more forward placement
- In males the "brighter" color is maintained since the vowels are not modified or covered as much at the high passaggio; rather the speech approach to singing is maintained
- Less resonance is used to enhance the speech approach to singing—the shape of the pharynx in speech is more relaxed than the stretched pharynx required in classical singing
- Vibrato is not always used or appropriate
- Chest register (mode 1, thyroarytenoid [TA] dominant, model voice) is used more than head register (mode 2, cricothyroid [CT] dominant, loft voice) in females
- Tessitura of songs mostly reside in the speech range of the voice

In addition, music theater voices, as with classical singers, have different colors, weights, and ranges. Some music theater singers use a darker and heavier production, which employs more chest than head register (chest/mix), while others employ a lighter, more head/mix combination. Often these choices are made based on the size of the instrument. A lighter-voiced music theater singer most often chooses a head/mix production, while the darker, heavier voices tend to choose the chest/mix sound. The chest/mix music theater voice usually has similarities to the classical alto or mezzo voice; the head/mix voice has similarities to the classical soprano.

BREATHING

If you're like most singers who work in or are seeking to work in music theater, it is more than likely that you have had, or are currently engaged in, some form of dance training. At this point, it's worth noting that breathing techniques for singing and dancing are different. Dancers, for example, are trained to pull in the abdominal muscles in order to create a strong center in the body for dance movement. This pulling in of the abdominal muscles often causes the intake of air to occur high in the lungs. The result is something we call clavicular breathing.

As a singer, however, you need to learn how to release some of these muscles for breathing when you sing. As part of your training, you'll practice this technique regularly until it comes naturally—no small challenge when singing *and* dancing!

We refer to this form of breathing as abdominal breathing, a standard breathing technique taught in classical singing. Regardless of genre—whether classical or music theater—the technique remains the same. As a music theater singer, it's worth your while to work from the same breathing concepts as classical singers who release the lower abdominals when they take in air. More specifically, in abdominal breathing the abdominals and rib cage expand comfortably with the intake of air. The ribs then maintain expansion during exhales and, with the upper body still, the abdominals slowly come in during exhale (what is called a controlled exhale).

Music theater actor, teacher, dancer, and director Donna Scheer describes breathing for dance as follows. Music theater singers need to maintain their lower core muscle support while dancing and simultaneously release the muscles in the midriff, waist, and lower back for singing. Scheer adds that postures change depending on the style of dance. For example, jazz dance posture is different than ballet posture. These adjustments need to be taken into account while singing to ensure that the support muscles are accessible while singing (Donna Scheer, personal communication, March 10, 2013).

Current voice science shows that less airflow is used in belt singing than in classical singing, since the closed phase of the glottis is longer in this style of singing. Since there are many weights of belt singing, the amount of airflow used varies: the lighter the belt singing, the more airflow is needed, since the closed phase of the glottis is shorter (Hall, 2006).

Breathing exercises are located on the NATS website, http://www.nats.org. Click on the "resources" tab and follow the instructions.

POSTURE

The alignment of the body for singing in music theater is just as important as in classical singing. Proper alignment (free of tension) of the head, neck, torso, arms, legs, and feet is directly related to breathing technique for both the music theater and classical singer. One exception to classical alignment is the position of the head: in belting, music theater singers often tilt their head up slightly to facilitate the upward movement of the larynx. In classical singing, the female also tips her head upward when singing in the whistle register (the C_7 range) (Hall, 2006).

REGISTERS

The use of chest and head register is the *defining difference* between female music theater and classical singing. In the simplest terms, female music theater singing requires more use of chest register, especially in the middle register (the middle-C octave), while classical singing uses more head register throughout the entire vocal range. Actually, there are multiple terms commonly used to describe the type of vocal fold vibration that occurs when you sing in chest register: mode 1, thyroarytenoid (TA) dominant, modal voice, light and heavy mechanism. Also, take a moment to read Dr. McCoy's description of registration on pages 31–34. For the sake of clarity and consistency, I will use the term *chest register* throughout this book. The development of a music theater female mix register creates a sung tone that is speech-like in character (Hall, 2006). Esteemed vocal pedagogues Cornelius L. Reid and William Vennard suggest using the terms "light mechanism" and "heavy mechanism" in place of "head register" and "chest register": "Thus we have two extremes of vibration, two 'registers' if you wish to call them that. One covers the lower two thirds of the compass and the other applies to the upper two thirds. I emphasize the fact that there is at least an octave which can be sung either way" (Vennard, 1967, 63).

Reid writes that the terms "heavy" and "light," when referring to head and chest registers, accurately describe the weight of the sound being sung. He also adds, "The important thing is not so much one's choice of terms, but knowing how to apply the functional principles which predispose the vocal folds to reflexively adjust to the desired configurations" (Reid, 1983, 146).

As discussed earlier in this book, Dr. Scott McCoy uses several terms to describe "chest register": mode 1, thyroarytenoid (TA) dominant, chest mode, or modal voice. As a singer you need to be aware of all these terms for describing the music theater singing voice since teachers and coaches use all of them. There is, however, a movement toward adopting the terms mode 1 (chest register) and mode 2 (head register) when describing the two modes of vocal fold vibration.

A female musical theater singer must be able to sing using a "soprano or legit, belt, and mix voice" (Balog, 2005, 402). The soprano or legit singing voice is most similar to classical singing except the color is brighter (Balog, 2005). Defining the registration of the belt voice is more difficult. Some voice teachers claim that belt singing is primarily a chest register or chest voice function that is used beyond the standard range of the chest register (above E_4) (Bevan, 1989; Balog, 2005; Hall, 2006; Roll, 2013). Other teachers argue that belting is an extension of the speaking voice, rather than chest register taken higher than the standard pitch range of approximately E_4. What is important to point out is that both chest register dominant singing and speaking use the throat muscle in a very similar way! So perhaps both claims about registration are correct since from a scientific standpoint, speaking and chest voice singing use a predominance of the same part of the vocal muscle, the thyroarytenoid.

Loud, brassy, nasal, bright, forward, and "ringy" are common words used to describe the belt sound. Before the advent of the pop/rock musical, the belt sound was mainly produced in the C_4–C_5 octave. The new pop/rock musicals, however, often require an extension of the mix/belt sound beyond the C_5 octave. These new demands mean singers have had to adjust their voices and techniques. The higher extension of the belt voice has several names: high belt, super belt, rock belt, and pop soprano (Sabella-Mills, 2010; Deer & Dal Vera, 2008; Roll, 2012). Often the belt voice is defined by what it is not: classical vocal production. It is generally accepted that the vocal demands of music theater singing are significantly different than classical singing technique.

Another way to understand the belt voice is that it is an extension of the speaking voice. Many teachers advocate the use of speech exercises to create the mix/belt sound. As a female music theater singer, you will sing in chest register (mode 1, TA dominant, modal voice) beyond the traditional classical shift at E or E flat above middle C. The goal of training in music theater is for you to develop the ability to carry chest register, in varying volumes, to the C above middle C and sometimes higher, if possible. To accomplish this, the development of a "mix" register is necessary. The term "mix" in music theater has a very different meaning than the classical term *voix mixte*, which is defined by vocal pedagogue Richard Miller as "the region of the singing voice in which sensations of 'chest' and 'head' are simultaneously experienced; the *zona di passaggio*" (Miller, 1992, 3). The music theater mix register is a blend of head and chest register with a predominance of chest register, whereas the *voix mixte* sound used in classical voice is a predominance of head register. It is possible (and very important) for you to develop the music theater mix, since it has a lighter and more spoken quality than belt singing, which is the sung extension of your "calling voice." In classical singing, the use or addition of "head" voice at the passaggio is increased more than in music theater singing. In short, music theater mix vocal production uses more chest register than does the classical *voix mixte*. The perceptual (aural) results, however, can be quite different, depending on the weight of voice. A lighter voice will have a different sound and weight when singing in mix and *voix mixte* than a heavier voice will have in both music theater and classical singing. Belting, which uses a maximum amount of thyroarytenoid (TA) muscle (chest register, mode 1, model voice), is used only on occasion, and usually at climactic points, in music theater. Rarely, if ever, will every note in a song be sung in belt production. There are exceptions, of course: a few music theater singers do use more belt than mix singing production with success. Voice scientists have not yet studied this phenomenon. The belt is often described as loud, brassy, nasal, and ringy. Up until ten to fifteen years ago, the mix/belt singing voice extended to C_5. With the recent arrival of the pop/rock style musical, a music theater female singer must now be able to produce the mix/belt sound to E_5 and beyond to meet the vocal requirements found in many of the new musicals like *Wicked* (2003).

Creating an appropriate balance between head and chest registers is of prime importance in music theater training. Some repertoires call for a head dominant mix sound, while others require a chest dominant mix sound. The use of head and chest mix registers also depends on the size of the voice. Lighter-voiced singers use more head mix quality; larger-voiced singers favor the chest mix quality. Most music theater singers use more head voice as they ascend in range, but rarely as much head voice as a classical singer uses (Hall, 2006).

One of the most effective ways for a female music theater singer to learn how to use her head and chest registers in music theater singing is to isolate both registers through exercises developed by Jeannette LoVetri, founder of Shenandoah University's Contemporary Commercial Music Vocal Pedagogy Institute (CCMVPI). In these exercises, you vocalize only in head register throughout your range and vocalize only in chest register where comfortable (LoVetri, 2004). Isolating your head register is best accomplished by starting at C_5-E_5 above middle C and exercising the voice down the scale to the lowest comfortable pitch, making sure you stay in head register. Chest register isolation in females is best accomplished at a comfortable pitch below middle C. Once your chest register is isolated, vocalize as high as is comfortable in chest register. Chest register taken above E_4 becomes your belt voice. When you can isolate the two registers, you can start learning to blend or mix them, remembering that the spoken quality and varying weights of chest register will dominate the sound. Often female music theater singers have difficulty staying in head voice from middle C_4 to the G_4 above it because they are accustomed to singing in their mix register at this pitch level. Because of that, it is very important to train your voice to stay in head voice to keep the muscles of the throat flexible and free of tension (LoVetri, 2004).

In music theater singing, as in classical singing, there are varying sizes of female voices. Consequently, the weight of the voice affects the size of the head, mix, and belt sounds. Often a heavier voice uses more chest register in the mix register and uses full belt singing at higher pitch levels and with more stamina. Stamina refers to the amount of time you can maintain a particular singing sound and remain vocally healthy and fresh without fatigue. The heavier voice often is more comfortable singing in belt register than in mix register. Heavy voices often display a head voice with a good deal of "noise" in the sound listening example. The lighter-weight voice is often more comfortable singing in mix register and uses belt register only sparingly or not at all. The light voice uses head voice often and with ease. In summary, the heavier voice tends to use more mix and belt registers, while lighter-weight voices tend to use more mix and head registers.

Some believe the mix/belt sound in music theater singing is created by a dominant use of chest register throughout the singing range, while others argue that adjusting the resonance of the voice to a brighter, more forward placement creates the mix/belt sound. In my experience, both are correct. In other words, adjusting the use of the vocal fold muscle and/or the resonance can create a music theater singing sound. I have also observed and am a firm believer that every singer must develop healthy head and chest register singing in order to create a balanced, health mix and to ensure vocal health and longevity.

Register exercises are located on the NATS website, http://www.nats. org. Click on the "resources" tab and follow the instructions.

TONE QUALITY ADJUSTMENT/RESONANCE

By changing where your voice resonates, you can achieve the brighter tone quality color often favored in music theater singing. The resonance adjustment can be used in conjunction with vocal fold function and adjustments. There are two actual resonators for the voice: the mouth/nasal cavity and the throat or pharyngeal cavity. The throat space resonance creates a darker tone quality color, and the mouth space resonance creates a brighter tonal quality singing color.

The contemporary music theater sound, which emphasizes the enunciation of the text rather than the beauty of the voice, results in singing that uses less resonance than classical production. Therefore, when a show is revived, the male and female roles are most often sung with a more contemporary sound. This change in singing styles also requires accompanying tone quality adjustments.

Tone quality is adjusted by changing the shape (mouth position) and/ or color (resonance position) of a vowel. Changing the shape of the vowel, in turn, changes the color of a sung tone to a more speech-like sound and alters the resonance qualities and space. These vowel adjustments are employed to clarify the text and ensure that the enunciation of the text predominates. The articulators (lips, tongue, jaw) shape differently for each vowel; it is this change in shape that is perceived by the ear as the brighter, more speech-like sound favored in music theater singing. Altering the shape of vowels to a more "forward" (but not nasal) placement and changing the shape of the mouth horizontally in a smile-like shape are two of the best ways to accomplish speech-like tone quality adjustment, as opposed to the stretched pharyngeal shape used in classical singing (Hall, 2006).

Because singing in music theater is electronically amplified, resonance requirements are not the same as in classical singing. Often the text or style in a music theater song calls for many different types of resonance, so consistent resonance throughout the voice is not necessary in music theater singing.

Resonance and vocal color exercises are located on the NATS website, http://www.nats.org. Click on the "resources" tab and follow the instructions.

RANGE

In general, the ranges of most music theater repertoire for females are lower than in classical singing. In some of the contemporary music theater repertoire, though, the ranges for men are often higher than in classical singing, encompassing the tenor, baritone, and bari-tenor *tessitura*. Many music theater composers are looking for "nonclassical" sounds such as falsetto and belt in the high range. Since music theater style is text dominant, a great deal of the repertoire for women and men is written in the middle range, facilitating the clear enunciation of the text.

Music theater publishers categorize female music theater repertoire as either soprano or alto/belter. Female music theater singers rarely use these labels, though. Instead, female music theater singers tend to categorize themselves as sopranos who can mix/belt. At auditions, female music theater singers are expected to sing a selection in their head register (Mode 2) and a selection in their mix/belt register (Mode 1). Consequently, voice teachers need to train singers to be flexible enough to sing well in both registers/modes.

In music theater, range and vocal color are not given the same emphasis as they are in classical vocal categories. Consequently, the distinction between the two female music theater vocal types is not as pronounced as that between the classical soprano and alto/mezzo vocal types and is usually based on registers rather than on classical vocal type descriptors. In music theater, the female voice is expected to sing repertoire in both the alto and soprano ranges, although the soprano *tessitura* is usually not as high as in the classical repertoire. In music theater, soprano voice and song require the singer to use more head register, while the alto/belter voice and song require more chest register. For example, often a light, high voice sings in the alto range and uses a predominance of chest register. Repertoire is usually described as "a soprano/head register piece" or a "mix/belt piece." Therefore, a low- or high-voiced singer needs to sing repertoire in both her head register and mix/belt register, depending on the demands of the style (Hall, 2006).

Historically, music theater repertoire has divided the male voice along the traditional classical baritone and tenor ranges. As with the women, though, the modern music theater repertoire blurs the line between high and low male voices. Men are expected to sing throughout the high and low ranges and with a variety of sounds: falsetto, belt, and a quasi-traditional classical sound. Therefore, the bari-tenor music theater voice type has emerged from the demands of the contemporary repertoire. The vocal requirements of the bari-tenor roles require an experienced performer and an advanced vocal technique.

CCM TEACHERS AND TEACHING "SYSTEMS"

Even though mix/belt singing is not new, formal training for mix/belt singing didn't really exist until recently. Degrees in music theater are a recent addition on college campuses. Traditionally, colleges that conferred degrees in classical music did not offer degrees in music theater singing. However, since 1970, many colleges, universities, and conservatories have begun offering programs in music theater. With the advent of voice science, more singers and teachers understand that mix/belt singing can be executed healthily. As a result, there are several teaching systems and teachers that specialize in mix/belt singing training. The following list is not meant to be inclusive: The Estill Voice Model, Somatic Voicework™ The LoVetri Method, Vocal Power Academy, Speech Level Singing Method, *Bel Canto Can Belto*, Robert Edwin Studio, and *Voiceworks*. It is worth your time to learn from all these approaches and teachers.

American voice teacher Jo Estill began researching her methods in 1979 and developed Estill Voice Training (EVT) in 1988. EVT is based on a three-part vocal system: power (lungs), source (vocal folds), and filter (vocal tract) and their application to a set of thirteen vocal exercises or "Figures for Voice." Training sessions are ongoing and offered worldwide.

Robert Edwin is a singer, songwriter, teacher, and author. His diverse performing career is matched by an equally diverse teaching career. He is one of the leading authorities on contemporary commercial music (CCM) and child voice pedagogy. He teaches at his independent studio in Cinnaminson, New Jersey, where classical singers interact with music theater performers, rock and pop vocalists, child singers, and pageant contestants. His DVD on child voice training, The Kid & the Singing Teacher, with CCC-SLP Barbara Arboleda, is an outstanding teaching tool. He authored a chapter on teaching children to sing for the 2008 book *Pediatric Voice Disorders* and is a chapter author for the 2012 *Handbook of Music Education* (Edwin, 2005–2013).

Somatic Voicework™ The LoVetri Method is a body-based method of vocal training, which draws from many disciplines. It is based upon voice science and medicine as well as traditional classical vocal training, complementary modalities such as yoga, movement, dance, acting, speech training, and various bodywork approaches (LoVetri, 2001–2013).

Elisabeth Howard created and developed the Vocal Power Method in Los Angeles, California. The method teaches and coaches all styles of singing and offers training materials, workshops, and private lessons.

Vocal coach Seth Riggs is the creator and founder of the Speech Level Singing Method, based in California.

Bel Canto Can Belto is an instructional DVD that teaches female music theater singing. It was developed and is taught by Mary Saunders-Barton, head of the voice department for the Penn State Music Theater Program. Her highly anticipated DVD *What About the Boys? Teaching Men to Sing Musical Theatre* will be released in 2014.

Singer and voice teacher Lisa Popeil created *Voiceworks, The Total Singer,* an instructional DVD, and *Sing Anything: Mastering Vocal Styles,* a book that teaches all vocal styles. Her *Voiceworks* studio is located in Sherman Oaks (Los Angeles), California.

Mary Saunders-Barton, a music theater voice specialist, teaches that a music theater singer must produce a "Vocal Arc" of sounds: "chest, speaking mix, soprano mix, head, and belt" (Berg, 2011, 374; Roll, 2012). The music theater mix/belt sound has a clear, communicative, nonclassical quality, and it has been heard onstage in America for more than one hundred years. Often because it sounds and seems so "natural," the need for training is ignored. Don't be fooled! Only since the 1970s have colleges and universities offered degrees and training in music theater singing. Even then, most teachers at the university level only have classical training. Take the time and effort to find a qualified teacher and coach. Study hard, practice regularly, and never stop training!

BIBLIOGRAPHY

Balog, J. E. (2005). A guide to evaluating music theater singing for the classical teacher. *Journal of Singing, 61*, 401–6.

Berg, G. (2011). Bel canto—can belto: Teaching women to sing musical theatre—Mary Saunders on belting and the mixed voice. *Journal of Singing, 67*, 373–75.

Bevan, R. V. (1989). Belting and chest voice: Perceptual differences and spectral correlates measures. Doctoral dissertation, Teachers College, Columbia University.

Deer, J., & Dal Vera, R. (2008). *Acting in musical theater: A comprehensive course.* New York: Routledge.

Doscher, B. (1994). *The functional unity of the singing voice*, 2nd edition. London: Scarecrow Press.

Edwin, R. (2005–2013). Robert Edwin Studio. Retrieved from http://robertedwinstudio.com/.

Green, S. (1980). *The world of musical comedy.* New York: Da Capo Press, Inc.

Hall, K. S. (2006). Music theater vocal pedagogy and styles: An introductory teaching guide for experienced classical singing teachers. Doctoral dissertation, Teachers College, Columbia University.

LoVetri, J. (2004). Handout from 2004 CCM Institute, Shenandoah University.

———. (2012). The confusion about belting: A personal observation. *Voice Prints 10*, 4–7.

LoVetri, J. (2001–2013). *Somatic Voicework*, the LoVetri method. Retrieved from http://www.thevoiceworkshop.com/somatic.html.

Miller, R. (1992). *Training tenor voices.* New York: Schirmer Books.

Reid, C. (1983). *A dictionary of vocal terminology.* New York: Joseph Patelson Music House, Ltd.

Roll, C. (2012). Musical theater singing in the 21st century: Examining the pedagogy of the female belt voice. Unpublished advanced proposal, Teachers College, Columbia University.

Sabella-Mills, D. (June 2010). Musical theater/CCM singing: Mechanics and acoustics of super-belt. Workshop presented at the New York Singing Teachers' Association's Professional Development Program, Teachers College, Columbia University.

Vennard, W. (1967). *Singing: The mechanism and the technique.* New York: Carl Fisher.

5

LISTENING EXAMPLES AND REPERTOIRE RECOMMENDATIONS

Music publishers most often categorize female music theater repertoire as either soprano or alto/belter. However, the female music theater singer rarely uses these labels. Instead, all female music theater singers categorize themselves as singers who sing in head register and their mix/belt register. At auditions, a female music theater singer is expected to sing a selection in their head register and a selection in their mix/belt register. Consequently, your training needs to be flexible enough to ensure that you can sing in your head register and mix/belt register. The distinction between the two female music theater vocal types is not as distinct as the classical soprano and alto/mezzo vocal types. In fact, it is quite different. In music theater, the female voice is expected to sing repertoire in both the alto and soprano range. However, the soprano range is usually not as high as in the classical repertoire. In music theater, the distinction between soprano and alto/belter is usually based on registers rather than classical vocal type descriptors. In music theater, "soprano" means a song that requires more use of head register, and the alto/belter register and songs require you to use more chest register. For example, often a light, high voice sings in the alto range and uses a predominance of chest register. Repertoire is described as "a soprano piece" or a "mix/belt piece." Therefore, regardless of whether you are a low- or high-voiced singer, you sing repertoire in both your head register and mix/belt register, depending on the demands of the style. In music theater, range and vocal color are not given the same emphasis as they are in classical vocal categories. Comprehension of the text is the most important factor in music theater singing production. Music theater singing is considered an extension of the speaking voice (Spivey, 2008). Female music theater belt and mix singing can be aurally perceived especially when compared to music theater and classical "legit" singing (Balog, 2005).

The traditional music theater repertoire divides the male voice along the traditional classical baritone and tenor ranges. As with the women, the modern music theater repertoire again blurs the line between high and low male voices. Men are expected to sing as high as possible and with a variety of sounds. Therefore, the bari-tenor music theater voice type has emerged from the demands of the contemporary repertoire. The bari-tenor roles require singing throughout the high and low range and often ask the male voice to produce a variety of vocal sounds: falsetto, belt, and a quasi-traditional classical sound. The vocal requirements of the bari-tenor roles require an experienced performer and an advanced vocal technique.

The contemporary sound, which emphasizes the enunciation of the text rather than the beauty of the voice, results in singing that uses less resonance than classical production. Therefore, there is an important caveat in male music theater singing: when a show is revived, the male (and female) roles are most often sung with a more contemporary sound.

One of the most important components in learning to sing and teach music theater singing is being able to hear and recognize the different sounds: head register, mix, and belt (examples are listed later in this chapter). All the listening examples cited can be found at the National Association of Teachers of Singing (NATS) website, http://www.nats.org. Select the "resources" link and follow the instructions. Each example contains the entire song and an excerpted portion. The excerpted portion contains the type of singing referenced. For clarification and ease of understanding, the definition(s) precede each type of singing example. The style of the musical example and the character type are also included with each singing example.

A sampling of vocalises you or your teacher can use to begin singing and teaching music theater voice is included, too. The exercises develop head, mix, chest, and belt singing. The exercises demonstrate how the head, mix, chest, and belt sounds can be applied to phrases excerpted from a music theater song. Again, refer to the NATS website, http://

www.nats.org, and select the "resources" link to hear the examples referenced below.

FEMALE BELT SINGING

Belt singing is female chest register sung in the octave above middle C and, on some occasions, at higher pitches. It is the dominant register of the belt voice. Chest register is the lowest register of the speaking voice. It is used for speaking and is created by the thicker part of the vocal folds: the thyroarytenoid (TA) muscle. Belt singing is often described as bright, brassy, full, and loud. Belt singing is speech based—an extension of the speaking voice. The speaking voice leads and dominates the singing voice; the two are blended. High belt is the term used to describe belt singing between C_4 and above. In classical singing, the chest register is not used as predominantly in the C_5 octave and above.

The higher pitches in these examples are representative of female belt singing.

Female Belt Singing Examples

1. (4:32–end) "Defying Gravity" from *Wicked* (pop style), sung by Idina Menzel (contemporary leading lady type)
2. (entire track) "Rafiki Mourns" from *The Lion King* (gospel/pop style), sung by Tsidii Le Loka (supporting gospel/pop type)
3. (1:44–1:50, 2:57–3:15) "When You're Good to Mama" from *Chicago* (jazz, pop style), sung by Queen Latifah (character type)
4. (2:17–2:26) "Days of Plenty" from *Little Women* (contemporary pop style), sung by Maureen McGovern (mature leading lady type)

MALE BELT SINGING

Male belt singing is a controversial and understudied field, with some experts claiming men belt and others believing they do not. One thing on which they all agree is that the male belt voice differs from the female mix/belt voice. Only the passaggio and above pitches are belted in the male music theater singer. At the high passaggio, the pharynx does not expand but stays in the speech position, and the vowels are not covered or modified. The low and middle ranges are not affected by the mix registration found in female music theater singers. The result is singing that is bright and speech-oriented in this region of the male music theater singer.

Male Belt Singing Examples

1. (2:11–end) "Man" from *The Full Monty* (pop/rock style), sung by Patrick Wilson (contemporary leading man type)
2. (2:20–end) "Mr. Greed" from *The Life* (jazz/rock style), sung by Sam Harris (contemporary leading man type)
3. (1:16–end) "Why? 'Cause I'm a Guy" from *I Love You, You're Perfect, Now Change* (pop style), sung by Danny Burstein and Robert Roznowski (mature leading man and contemporary leading man types)

FEMALE AND MALE CHARACTER VOICE SINGING

Male and female character voice roles are found in both music theater and opera. In music theater, character voice singing requires the altering of one's voice to communicate the perceived personality of the character portrayed. Most character voices are comic roles. The vocal quality is chosen to emulate the character and is expressed in an exaggerated fashion.

Female Character Voice Singing Example

1. (entire track or 0:35–1:08) "Adelaide's Lament" from *Guys and Dolls* (jazz/rock style), sung by Vivian Blaine (character type)

Male Character Voice Singing Example

1. (1:10–end) "I Really Like Him" from *Man of La Mancha* (historic, operetta style), sung by Ernie Sabella (character type)

FEMALE MIX SINGING

Mix register in music theater describes a female singing sound that is a blend of head and chest registers used to create the various styles of the belt sound. Twangy, ringy, and pop soprano are used to describe the mix sound. The sound can be head register dominant with some chest or chest dominant with some head register. This mix blend can occur at any pitch level. Mix register is sometimes referred to as "blended" or "coordinated" register.

Chest mix is singing that is not pure chest register production. The chest register dominates, but a small amount of head register is also present. It differs from classical singing in that the amount of chest voice used at any pitch level is more significant than in classical production.

Head mix is female music theater singing that is not pure head register production. The head register dominates, but a small amount of chest register is also present. It differs from classical singing in that the amount of chest voice used at any pitch level is more significant than in classical production.

Female Mix Singing

1. (2:06–2:59) "The Sacred Bird" from *Miss Saigon* (pop/rock style), sung by Lea Salonga (contemporary leading lady type)
2. (0:11–1:14) "Better" from *Little Women* (pop style), sung by Sutton Foster (contemporary leading lady type)
3. (entire track) "Popular" from *Wicked* (pop/rock style), sung by Kristin Chenoweth (contemporary leading lady type)

"LEGIT" MUSIC THEATER SINGING

"Legit," a slang term shortened from the word *legitimate*, is used in music theater to describe male and female classical singing. There are two types of legit singing: traditional and contemporary. The traditional legit sound has the qualities of classical singing; the contemporary legit sound, while head-voice dominant, is more speech oriented. The speech component in contemporary legit singing results in a vocal sound that employs less classical resonance and has a brighter quality, as opposed to the darker quality found in the traditional legit sound. It is a head register dominant vocal production that is similar to female classical singing.

Female Contemporary Legit Singing Examples

1. (beginning–1:26) "I Won't Mind" from *The Other Franklin* (pop style), sung by Audra McDonald (contemporary leading lady type)
2. (3:33–end) "Think of Me" from *The Phantom of the Opera* (pop opera style), sung by Sarah Brightman (contemporary leading lady type)

Male Contemporary Legit Singing Examples

1. (0:44–1:12) "How I Am" from *Little Women* (pop style), sung by John Hickok (contemporary leading man type)
2. (0:59–1:36) "I Confess" from *Footloose* (pop/rock style), sung by Stephen Lee Anderson (mature contemporary leading man type)
3. (0:36–1:42) "Shouldn't I Be Less in Love with You?" from *I Love You, You're Perfect, Now Change* (pop style), sung by Robert Roznowski (contemporary leading man type)

FEMALE AND MALE CLASSICAL MUSIC THEATER SINGING

Singing in the classical style is rarely heard on the Broadway stage today, especially in the male voice. The classical examples cited here are included for historical interest and for comparison to the contemporary legit sound commonly used today.

Female Classical Music Theater Singing Examples

1. (entire track) "What's the Use of Wond'rin'" from *Carousel* (historical, operetta style), sung by Shirley Jones (historical leading lady type)
2. (entire track) "Waitin' for My Dearie" from *Brigadoon* (historical, operetta style), sung by Marion Bell (historical leading lady type)

Male Classical Music Theater Singing Examples

1. (entire track) "The Impossible Dream" from *Man of La Mancha* (historical, operetta style), sung by Brian Stokes Mitchell (historical leading man type)
2. (entire track) "Some Enchanted Evening" from *South Pacific* (historical, operetta style), sung by Ezio Pinza (historical leading man type)

EXERCISES FOR DEVELOPING MUSIC THEATER SINGING

The exercises in the section are selected from my own teaching and from many of the prominent music theater singing teachers: Mary Saunders-Barton, Robert Edwin, Jeannette LoVetri, Lisa Popeil, Elisabeth Howard, and others. Please visit the NATS website at http://www.nats.organd click on the "resources" tab to hear these examples.

1. Head register/light mechanism/mode two.
2. Chest register/heavy mechanism/mode one.
3. Mix register: a blend of light and heavy mechanism/head and chest register/mode one and two. Once you are able to isolate head, chest, and mix registers, it is helpful to alternate between mix and head register in the comfortable part of your range.
4. Chest/mix register: a blend of light and heavy mechanism, heavy dominates.
5. Belt: a dominance chest register/heavy mechanism/mode one.

"HISTORICAL" REPERTOIRE RECOMMENDATIONS FOR EACH VOICE TYPE

Recommended "historical" introductory repertoire for each voice type is listed below. Historical repertoire refers to selections mostly from the pre-1960s era of music theater. The historical selections require the use of a more "legit" or head dominant vocal production. Several song selections for soprano, alto/belter, tenor, and baritone are provided below. The title, show, style, and tempo are listed for each song.

Soprano/Head Register

1. "How Could I Ever Know" from *The Secret Garden* (pop opera style), Contemporary Legit/Ballad, leading lady type
2. "Far From the Home I Love" from *The Fiddler on the Roof* (historical and jazz style), Legit/Ballad, historical ingénue type
3. "I Feel Pretty" from *West Side Story* (historical and jazz style), Legit/Up-tempo, historical ingénue type
4. "Cockeyed Optimist" from *South Pacific* (historical operetta style), Legit/Up-tempo, historical ingénue type

Alto/Mix/Belt

1. "Anyone Can Whistle" from *Anyone Can Whistle* (contemporary historic style), Mix/Ballad, contemporary leading lady type
2. "In My Own Little Corner" from *Cinderella* (historical operetta style), Mix/Ballad, historical ingénue type
3. "I Cain't Say No" from *Oklahoma* (historical operetta style), Mix/Belt/Up-tempo, historical character type
4. "I'm Gonna Wash That Man Right Out of My Hair" from *South Pacific* (historical operetta style), Mix/Belt/Up-tempo, ingénue type

Tenor

1. "We Kiss in a Shadow" from *The King and I* (historical operetta style), Legit/Ballad, male ingénue type
2. "Younger Than Springtime" from *South Pacific* (historic operetta style), Legit/Ballad, leading man type
3. "Kansas City" from *Oklahoma* (historic operetta style), Contemporary with country accent/Up-tempo, character type
4. "You Mustn't Kick it Around" from *Pal Joey* (jazz style), Contemporary Legit/Up-tempo, leading man type

Baritone

1. "The Surrey With the Fringe on Top" from *Oklahoma* (historical operetta style), Legit/Up-tempo, historical leading man type
2. "Johanna" from *Sweeney Todd* (contemporary historical style), Contemporary Legit/Ballad, contemporary ingénue type
3. "Empty Chairs at Empty Tables" from *Les Miserables* (pop opera style), Contemporary Legit/Ballad, contemporary ingénue type
4. "Luck Be a Lady" from *Guys and Dolls* (pop jazz style), Contemporary Legit/Up-tempo, historical leading man type

CONTEMPORARY REPERTOIRE RECOMMENDATIONS FOR EACH VOICE TYPE

Several song selections for soprano, alto/belter, tenor, and baritone voice types are provided below. The title, show, style, and tempo are listed for each song. All these songs require a more advanced vocal technique. These examples are representative of the popular vocal sound that you will want to be taught. Since the repertoire is current and constantly changing, it can be challenging for music theater singers and teachers to remain current in their field.

Soprano/Head Register/Mix-Belt

1. "Somewhere That's Green" from *Little Shop of Horrors* (pop style), Mix/Ballad, contemporary/pop leading lady type
2. "Feelings" from *The Apple Tree* (contemporary historical style), Mix-Belt/Up-tempo, young female ingénue type
3. "A Change in Me" from *Beauty and the Beast* (pop style), Mix/Ballad, young female ingénue type
4. "Don't Nobody Bring Me No Bad News" from *The Wiz* (rhythm and blues style), Mix-Belt/Up-tempo, African American comic character type
5. "The Beauty Is" from *The Light in the Piazza* (pop opera style), Head Mix/Moderate Up-tempo, contemporary ingénue leading lady type

Alto/Mix-Belt

1. "Christmas Lullaby" from *Songs for a New World* (pop/rock style), Mix-belt/Ballad, contemporary pop leading lady type
2. "Nothing Really Happened" from *Is There Life After High School?* (pop style), Mix/Ballad, young female ingénue type
3. "Someone Else's Story" from *Chess* (pop style), Mix-belt/Ballad, contemporary pop leading lady type
4. "Take Me to the World" from *Evening Primrose* (contemporary historical style), Mix/Up-tempo, contemporary pop leading lady type
5. "Show Off" from *The Drowsy Chaperone* (contemporary historical style), Mix/Up-tempo, contemporary pop leading lady type

Tenor

1. "No Moon" from *Titanic* (pop opera style), Contemporary Legit/Ballad, young male ingénue type
2. "Johanna" from *Sweeney Todd* (contemporary historical style), Contemporary Legit-Falsetto/Ballad, young male ingénue type
3. "The Kid Inside" from *Is There Life After High School?* (pop style), Contemporary Pop Rock-Belt/Up-tempo, young male ingénue type
4. "Something's Coming" from *West Side Story* (contemporary historical and jazz style), Contemporary Legit-Belt/Up-tempo, young male ingénue type
5. "Left Behind" from *Spring Awakening* (contemporary pop/rock style), Contemporary Pop Rock-Falsetto/Ballad, young male ingénue type

Baritone

1. "Lost in the Stars" from *Lost in the Stars* (contemporary historical style), Contemporary Legit/Ballad, African American mature leading man type
2. "It's Hard to Speak My Heart" from *Parade* (pop rock style), Contemporary Legit-Belt/Ballad, contemporary pop leading man type

3. "Les Poissons" from *Little Mermaid* (pop style), Character Voice/ Up-tempo, comic character type
4. "Comedy Tonight" from *A Funny Thing Happened on the Way to the Forum* (contemporary historical style), Contemporary Legit-Belt/Up-tempo, comic character
5. "All That's Known" from *Spring Awakening* (contemporary pop/ rock style), Contemporary Legit-Mix/Up-tempo, contemporary pop male ingénue type

BIBLIOGRAPHY

Balog, J. E. (2005). A guide to evaluating music theater singing for the classical teacher. *Journal of Singing, 61*, 401–6.
Spivey, N. (2008). Music theater singing . . . let's talk. Part 2: Examining the debate on belting. *Journal of Singing, 64*, 607–14.

6

MUSIC THEATER STYLES

In addition to learning about music theater history and the mechanics of singing in the music theater style and being able to identify the various music theater singing sounds, another challenge facing music theater singers and teachers is developing a thorough understanding of the many styles found in the music theater song literature, then learning how to sing those varied styles. There are two basic ways to categorize music theater styles: vocal/singing type (head, mix, belt) and style type (pop, rock, country, etc.). In this chapter listening examples are included to help you hear the various styles and sound. All listening examples can be found at the NATS website, http://www.nats.org. Click on the "resources" tab and follow the instructions.

Renowned singer, composer, teacher, and writer Robert Edwin has a broad overall understanding of this area and the performance experience to back it up. The versatile "Bach to Rock" artist and teacher suggests that, for vocal teachers and coaches who have Broadway type singers in their studios, "the challenge is to identify and understand the various vocal styles used in musicals and then produce the vocal technique, performance skills, and repertoire necessary to develop those styles that the singers wish to sing and/or are capable of singing" (Edwin, 2003, 432).

If you're a singer, you'd better be prepared to tackle just about *anything* when you show up for an audition. For instance, LoVetri (2003) notes the variety of singing styles requested in an edition of *Backstage*, a newspaper devoted to music theater news and casting calls:

- Come prepared with a pop sound
- Must belt to D
- Singer must be able to mix
- Prepare a forties and funky R and B tune
- Females come prepared to sing an Ella Fitzgerald–style swing number
- A Mahalia Jackson–style gospel number
- A seventies R and B selection

Eleven years later, however, the vocal requirements have continued to change. The introduction of the pop/rock musical style has created new demands for a music theater singer (Roll, 2012). In the April 2011 issue of *Backstage*, audition requirements called for:

- Pop/rock singer, good belt range
- Must have a great pop/contemporary musical theater voice with a high belt
- 20s–30s, seeking a high belter with strong soprano
- Needs a thrilling singing voice with high soprano and belt capability
- Great singer with R and B and riffing skills
- Female, pop/rock voice

American ragtime pianist, composer, actor, and author Max "Ragtime Man" Morath (2002) offers a historical context for those music theater styles. "Neat lines of development are impossible to discern in the history of American music theater," he writes in his book *Popular Standards*. "The American music theater contains influences from jazz, Vaudeville, burlesque, revues, ragtime, the blues, jazz, and operetta" (18). The music theater repertoire is rich with examples of all these styles, and often more than one style is found in songs from music theater shows—rock/pop, poperetta, folk/country, and more (Hall, 2006).

In the past few years, music theater vocal pedagogue LoVetri and others have favored the blanket term contemporary commercial music (CCM) to refer to any type of nonclassical singing, including cabaret, country, folk, gospel, jazz, rock, pop, rap, rhythm and blues, alternative, and experimental, along with, of course, music theater (LoVetri and Weekly, 2002). Most of those CCM categories can be found in the music theater repertoire at any given time. Therefore, she says, "Addressing these styles appropriately is very important" (LoVetri, 2013), along with the fact that most of them originated in this country:

> One of the reasons why vocal training aimed at music as it was sung in the sixteenth to nineteenth centuries is not a good match for the CCM styles is because the classical styles were commissioned and supported by royalty, aristocracy, and the church. The formal, elegant compositional conventions of those centuries are far away from the free wheeling origins of our own musical diversity. Over the last 150 or so years, CCM styles were derived from simple, ordinary folks who settled in various geographic areas in the United States, and created music to suit their own needs and interests. (LoVetri, 2013, 82)

Each individual CCM style is broad, distinctive, and the result of many decades of development. Conversely, while the styles are distinctly different, similarities and overlap occur in music theater songs and shows. In the following sections, you will learn the characteristics of each style and the corresponding performance practices of each. If you want to sing effectively in these styles, you need to study each one and become familiar with their unique stylistic characteristics, as well as the accompanying vocal production attributes necessary to meet the stylistic demands (Hall, 2006).

Music theater is complex and can be challenging to understand because it encompasses all styles from classical ("legit") music through rock 'n' roll, and the styles from older eras are often commingled with newer styles in both revivals and new productions. The "legit" vocal style must also be included as a music theater style. The term "legit," when used by Broadway singers, is a shorthand term for "legitimate" and means a sound sung in the classical style, employing more head than chest voice throughout the range (Edwin, 2003). The characteristics of legit singing include *chiaroscuro* fullness, clarity of vowels and consonants, evenness of tone quality throughout range, notes more sung than spoken, and a consistent vibrato. The legit style has its roots in the classical and operetta singing tradition; in fact, most music theater productions before the 1960s used this type of vocal production. It reached its pinnacle in the scores by Rodgers and Hammerstein. Put another way, the older shows (pre-1960) retain the vocal values of a more classical tradition (LoVetri, 2002).

Lyrics and story line drive singing in music theater more than does the singing itself, as is often the case in classical singing. Often contemporary singers must not only be able to sing in a wide variety of vocal qualities, but also be excellent actors and move well to music, even if they are not, strictly speaking, dancers (LoVetri, 2013). "The performance must always be delivered in an honest and committed manner and sung in the vocal quality appropriate to the role and the character with accepted stylistic embellishments" (LoVetri, 2013, 83).

In order to sing the wide variety of styles in a stylistically appropriate way, you need to know which styles require belt, mix, head, or a combination of those singing sounds. In addition, the styles and vocal choices are in a constant state of flux, a reflection of the current demands and tastes of the ever-changing music business.

Music theater is unique because it is the only singing genre that asks for specific pitch ranges for a particular vocal quality. Casting calls often list very specific vocal ranges and qualities: "belt to E_5," "mix to G_5," "legit range to B_6." For decades it has been expected that music theater singers can sing in all these qualities (head, mix, belt) easily and well. When you audition for a role, you need to know what each of these descriptions actually sounds like and how to sing them. Each requires a different technique, and they are not interchangeable, so you need to be able to hear and sing the distinctions. Consequently, training for music theater must include exercises to strengthen each type of singing until it is balanced against the others. Remember, too, that not all songs are appropriate for all singers; you must gauge the difficulty level of the song to your current ability. For example, if you are a very young singer and want to sing "Defying Gravity" from *Wicked*, you might be wise to wait until you are older before tackling this challenging piece (LoVetri, 2013).

MUSIC THEATER SINGING STYLES

As mentioned earlier, another way for you to understand the music theater voice is by dividing the singing into pedagogical categories. Edwin (2003), one of the leading music theater teachers, uses a system of four vocal categories: traditional legit, contemporary legit, traditional belt, and contemporary belt. Singers are often required to use one or more of these styles in the same musical, or sometimes even the same song (Edwin,

2003). In order to show how these categories historically have been associated with musicals, let's look back at the 2003 Broadway season. During that year, twenty-one musicals ran on Broadway: seven "revivals" and fourteen "new" productions. A revival is a show that has previously been produced on Broadway, had an extended run, and has been closed for some time. New shows are debut productions of music theater works that have never before been mounted on Broadway. The vocal styles found in those twenty-one productions ranged from classical all the way to rock (Edwin, 2003).

The Broadway legit sound is divided into traditional and contemporary legit categories: the traditional legit sound is more classically oriented, while contemporary legit is more speech-like and less formal (Edwin, 2003). The contemporary legit sound can contain classical elements, but also can include pop- and rock-influenced characteristics (Edwin, 2003). Oftentimes, when a traditional legit show is revived, a more contemporary legit sound is used (Edwin, 2003). Examples of traditional and contemporary legit shows from that 2003 season include *Man of La Mancha, Cabaret, Les Miserables, Flower Drum Song,* and *Phantom of the Opera* (Edwin, 2003).

In the female voice, the belt style uses a more chest dominant sound and a speech-like approach to singing. You can find examples of female belt singing in chapter 5. The male belt requires a narrowing and brightening of the classical sound and a more speech-like approach and phrasing (Edwin, 2003). Male belting listening examples are referenced in chapter 5. Traditional belt refers to the sound favored before the 1960s introduction of rock and roll–style Broadway musicals and contains some contemporary legit production as well. *Chicago, Cabaret, Flower Drum Song, Into the Woods,* and *The Producers* are examples of traditional belt shows from 2003 (Edwin, 2003). Listening examples are referenced in chapter 5.

Contemporary belt includes many additional vocal sounds such as slides, slurs, noises, melismatic runs, shrieks, and screams. The vocal quality is also varied and includes breathy, whiney, nasal, and raspy. The belt range is often extended as high as the singer is capable of producing. *Aida, Hairspray, Les Miserables, The Lion King,* and *Mamma Mia* are all examples of 2003 shows that required the use of the contemporary belt sound (Edwin, 2003) and listening examples are referenced in chapter 5.

The styles associated with music theater singing range from country, folk, gospel, jazz/swing, pop, and rock, to rhythm and blues. The purest forms of these styles are defined below, along with examples of music theater shows employing each style. (Of course, the pure form of the styles is rarely found in music theater singing.) As expert teacher Mary Saunders-Barton explains, "The styles that you have mentioned are pure forms. They are not music theater forms. They are created from the way the music expresses itself—the composer chooses that. The actual way the actors sing tends not to be toward the pure forms." She goes on to add that it is important for teachers to listen and understand the pure forms, so they "get them in their ear" (Mary Saunders-Barton, personal communication, April 5, 2006). The same could be said for singers.

COUNTRY STYLE AND SINGING

Country music is a style of popular music that traces its origins to many diverse sources—country dance tunes, archaic ballads of Anglo-Saxon and Celtic origins, nineteenth-century popular song, African American blues and gospel, and sacred music from the numerous religious revivals begun in the eighteenth century (Tribe, 2001). Country music has a rich history going back to the beginnings of the twentieth century in the United States, and it is important to familiarize yourself with many of its past and present stars, such as Hank Williams, Patsy Cline, Johnny Cash, and Dolly Parton (LoVetri, 2013).

Country singing is characterized by high pitch, tense control, and nasal tone (Middleton, 2000). Tense control refers to the placement of sound and pharynx shape—the vowels are sung very forward in the "mask," and the shape of the pharynx is relaxed and sometimes tight rather than stretched as in classical singing. A good example of the "tension" descriptor is heard in the recordings of the first great country solo singer, Jimmie Rodgers, as well as in those of country singer/songwriter Hank Williams (Middleton, 2000). The most common instruments used in country and western music are guitar, banjo, fiddle, mandolin, dobro, steel guitar, and sometimes bass and drums, while the major musical elements are a straightforward chord progression, a resonating chorus or bridge, numerous variations on a theme, and a style of fiddle playing with distinct sounds found in Scottish and Irish fiddle music. The lyrics tend to be about love, are often funny, and generally tell a memorable story (Gammond, 1991).

The country singing found in music theater today has its roots in the commercialization of country and western found in movies featuring "screen cowboys" such as Gene Autry and Roy Rogers. The western and western swing music they sang was, for the most part, performed in the compositional style of the Golden Age and Tin Pan Alley era (Gammond, 1991). At the same time, country singers Dolly Parton and Roger Miller created their unique sounds combining elements of country with pop. "By the 1950s there was a clear divide between the authentic school . . . and in the wider folk music field, the country music which became a part of the commercial world of pop/country fusion" (Gammond, 1991, 134).

Country singing breathing patterns and lung pressures are similar to those found in speech, and country singing is often described as more similar to normal speech than is classical singing. In the higher range, country singers tend to employ "pressed" phonation (long, closed phases of glottal adduction), and they tend to avoid pressed phonation in the lower range and at softer dynamic levels (Sundberg, 2000).

Country and folk music share some of the same roots and also have many stylistic elements in common. Both styles call for singing that is speech oriented, storytelling in character, distinctive in vocal quality, often twangy, not dependent on resonance, and with little vibrato. Yodeling is another distinctive characteristic of country singing, most often used when singing a pitch from chest register to head register.

Examples of musicals requiring country singing are *Shenandoah* (1974) by Geld and Udell; *Best Little Whorehouse in Texas* (1978) by Hall, King, and Masterson; *Big River* (1985) by Miller and Hauptman; and *Cowgirls* (1996) by Mufitt. Some country singers that belt healthily are KD Lang, Carrie Underwood, and Martina McBride.

FOLK STYLE AND SINGING

Folk music is a broad and elusive term, and musicologists still argue over its diffuse and somewhat nebulous origins (Gammond, 1991). One thing all the various folk styles have in common, however, is that the music typically has been shared and performed by an entire community (not by just a special class of expert performers), and usually has been transmitted by word of mouth, rather than via notation (Answers.com, retrieved July 4, 2013). This music "by and of the people" has evolved from many folk traditions, within widespread geographical locations and in different historical periods. It exemplifies, both covertly and overtly, class, nationalistic background, and ethnic identity, arising from and surviving in societies not yet affected by mass communication and the commercialization of culture. Because of this diversity, the essential nature of folk music continues to be a controversial subject. In fact, says musicologist and author Peter Gammond, "It could be said that all popular music is folk-music" (1991, 198).

During the 1960s and 1970s, folk music experienced a popular revival, led by the Kingston Trio; Peter, Paul and Mary; Bob Dylan; Joan Baez; and others, and it still has many practitioners and fans today (About.com).

The folk music singing range is mostly that of the spoken voice and tends to be sung in a simple, direct, speech-like manner. The musical and lyrical structure is usually simple and is often performed as an incantation style that suggests little or no structure (Gammond, 1991). Vocal ballads, whether they are about love, religion, work, war, or death, are the most common form of folk music. Ballads are typified by their uncomplicated musical and harmonic patterns and their simple, beautiful melodies. Often folk music replicates a cultural dialect in performance and shows structural influences from the classical, religious, and secular music of the culture from which it originates. A folk singer needs to be able to sing with accurate intonation, a reasonable amount of range, and clear pronunciation, but the "folksy" individuality of the performer has an impact on all of these factors.

The music theater show examples for both the country and folk styles are the same, since country music is one form of the folk style, and both styles are intertwined in music theater history: *Shenandoah* (1974) by Geld and Udell; *Best Little Whorehouse in Texas* (1978) by Hall, King, and Masterson; *Big River* (1985) by Miller and Hauptman; and *Cowgirls* (1996) by Mufitt. This intertwining is not unusual, as most contemporary musicals can be characterized as having a combination of two or more styles.

GOSPEL AND RHYTHM AND BLUES STYLES
AND SINGING

Gospel music traces its roots to three main sources: the freestyle improvised collections of worship music from the African American Christian
Church congregations, spirituals from the 1850s, and the rhetorical
speech patterns of the gospel preacher (Dorthea Taylor, personal communication, March 10, 2006). Rhythm and blues is a form of popular music
of African American origin that evolved from blues and jazz during the
1940s. Both the gospel and rhythm and blues styles have many similarities, as well as differences. The most significant difference concerns the
text: rhythm and blues can be said to be the secular version of gospel
(Taylor, 2006).

Gospel singing in African American churches is often characterized as
"fervent" and has been influenced by the blues and later by the jazz style.
When gospel music first emerged from African American churches in the
1930s, it was considered an offshoot of the jazz style and was mostly
known and appreciated only in those circles (Gammond, 1991). The mi-
gration of African Americans—and their music—from rural farms and
plantations to the urban centers starting after the Civil War greatly influenced the gospel style, and today gospel enjoys worldwide popularity
(Taylor, 2006).

In gospel singing, the emotion expressed by the singer is deeply personal and devotional and often overshadows the text. In many gospel
songs, each repetition of the text is improvised or ornamented differently
and sung with an increasing and varied outcry of emotion. Interestingly,
similar characteristics are found in Mozart's *Alleluia* and the music of
Handel and the Baroque era, the same text repeatedly sung with emotional variety, color, and ornamentation based on improvisation of the melody (Robert Edwin, personal communication, January 24, 2006).

Rhythm and blues has the same emphasis on emotions, uses similarly
extensive range, and also adds ornate vocal embellishments based on
chord progressions. In rhythm and blues, though, there is a wider variance
in volume from soft to very loud. The rhythm and blues style has also
been influenced by elements of the rock style, and vice versa (LoVetri,
2002). Gospel and rhythm and blues eventually merged with the pop style
in the 1960s and 1970s through artists such as the Drifters and the Jackson Five (Gammond, 1991). For many people, this amalgam sound was

best typified as the "Motown" sound, after music that emerged from Detroit (the Motor City).

Much of the gospel music repertoire requires a mature and healthy singing technique because the music is often robust and demanding. Singers beware: If you do not understand the demands of the music and what your voice and technique are capable of doing, you could experience vocal difficulties.

To review, while gospel and rhythm and blues share many characteristics, they also have their differences, as shown in this list (Hall, 2006):

Gospel Elements

- Sacred text
- Great deal of body movement
- Pronounced vibrato
- Emotional and energetic expression of words and music
- Simple melodies
- Highly improvised and ornamented
- Wide vocal range
- Big, heavy use of voice employing belt singing

Rhythm and Blues elements

- Secular text
- Often less vibrato
- Tone is often husky, rough, raspy
- Highly ornamented melodies
- Lighter use of voice
- Uniqueness and individuality of vocal timbre important

Musicals well known for employing both gospel and rhythm and blues styles of singing are *Purlie* (1970) by Geld and Udell; *Gospel at Colonus* (1985) by Breuer; *Dreamgirls* (1981) by Krieger and Eyen; *The Color Purple* (2005) by Russell, Willis, and Bray; and *The Wiz* (1974) by Smalls and Brown. Singers Jennifer Hudson, Queen Latifah, Bonnie Raitt, and Bessie Smith are a few outstanding examples of rhythm and blues/soul/gospel belt singers.

JAZZ AND SWING STYLES AND SINGING

Characteristics of the jazz style are often used when singing music theater repertoire, so becoming familiar with this style is important for singers and teachers. Jazz is a musical world in and of itself, with a unique set of parameters. Because music is the most important element of jazz (LoVetri, 2002), words are often replaced by "scatting." *The New Grove Dictionary of Jazz* defines scatting as: "A technique of jazz singing in which onomatopoetic or nonsense syllables are sung to improvised melodies" (515). Famous scat singers include Louis Armstrong, Jon Hendricks, and Ella Fitzgerald.

Another common device used in jazz singing is "bending" notes, which means deliberately singing above or below the pitch as an expressive device (Cooper, 2003; LoVetri, 2002). Often in jazz singing, less volume is used than that found in Broadway or classical singing, but any volume is appropriate, since originality and uniqueness of sound are the characteristics most valued (Cooper, 2003; LoVetri, 2002).

One way you can learn how to sing and teach in the jazz style is by listening to the great jazz singers. Although jazz is an American invention, examples of the jazz style exist worldwide and have evolved for the past hundred years into a diverse form based on improvisation. As a general rule, the singers are most often female ("songbirds"), and the instrumentalists are mostly male, although women are becoming more common players in jazz combos these days. Jazz singers are most highly regarded for their uniqueness of sound and ability to improvise. Phrasing, accurate intonation, melodic freedom, and control are all trademarks of a good jazz singer. Loud, powerful singing is not usually a part of the jazz vocal idiom, since the use of a microphone and sound system are key components of most jazz performances. The jazz ensemble—usually consisting of the basic jazz trio: piano, bass, and drums, and often including trumpet, saxophone, and/or other solo instruments—almost always involves a statement of the melody followed by the trading of "riffs" (improvised solos) inspired by the playing of their fellow musicians. One jazz term for this kind of call-and-response (a gospel term) interplay is "trading eights." Jazz singers are trained to understand the sometimes complex harmonic progressions, scales, chords, and rhythms specific to jazz theory, which then serve as the map and source of their creative expression (LoVetri, 2013).

What gives jazz its distinctive sound is thrusting, energetic rhythms, syncopated melodies, and an improvisational character (Gammond, 1991). The jazz style, according to Gammond, "is assumed to be of black origin and first emerged in the USA in various modified strains at the end of the 19th century" (290). Another way to understand and teach the jazz style is to listen to one or more successful jazz singers, including Armstrong, Billie Holiday, Nat "King" Cole, Fitzgerald, Sarah Vaughan, and Joe Williams. LoVetri describes the magic of Fitzgerald this way:

> She could be breathy, nasal, or clear in tone quality, deep and warm, light and delicate, or brassy and raucous in vocal quality. She was comfortable from very soft to very loud, from one end of her long range to another, at any speed from slow to fast. She was known for a remarkable intonation that never faltered. Sometimes Fitzgerald could change so much from song to song that her voice became almost unrecognizable. Truly, this was an instrument of great flexibility and strength, but not the same kind of flexibility and strength as that of a classical singer. (LoVetri, 2002, 250)

Another feature of the jazz style is the "lead sheet," from which jazz singers often learn their notes and rhythms. A lead sheet provides the melody, lyrics, and chord symbols, but there is no written-out accompaniment. Although jazz singers learn from a lead sheet, they use these notes and rhythms only as a point of departure when performing, taking what is written on the page or lead sheet and turning it into a personal theme with their own variations (Cooper, 2003). This practice can be highly useful in music theater, since most vocal parts are written in the lead sheet format, and singers often use the same process for performing most other contemporary styles found in the music theater repertoire (Hall, 2006).

Another important component of successful jazz singing is the concept of "space" (Cooper, 2003). The most basic definition of space is that every note written on the page can serve as a point of departure. Space has several characteristics: the pitch can be changed either up or down while respecting the harmony; the note can become more than one note (ornaments, repeated notes, etc.); the note can be started earlier or later than written; and the duration of notes can be changed (Cooper, 2003). Frank Sinatra was both a jazz and a pop singer and was especially adept at using the latter two embellishments to sing "in front of" or "behind" the beat. Peckham (2003) uses the term "embellishment" to describe the jazz style of making changes in the melody and rhythm of a piece.

A jazz singer can also choose to alter the structure, rhythm, key, and/ or genre of a jazz piece. For instance, with an AABA compositional form, the singer could start at the B section or any other section instead of at the beginning. Alternatively, a ballad could be performed as a bossa nova simply by changing the rhythm of the melody and accompaniment to reflect a bossa nova rhythm, or a swing tune could be reinvented as a blues. The possibilities are as endless as the imagination and "chops" of the jazz musicians. A change in the rhythm can also change the character of a piece: a tune in 3/4 time, for example, can take on a new character by shifting the time signature to 4/4 (Cooper, 2003).

Swing is a style of jazz that emerged during the early 1930s (the Swing Era) and flourished through the Big Band Era until about 1945. Swing music has always been closely associated with swing dancing, including the Lindy Hop, jive, bop, and, yes, swing. Swing has been called "the most debated word in jazz." As Cooper (2003) points out, "Swing is difficult to explain yet it is the defining characteristic of popular and jazz styles" (154). Nonetheless, the *Britannica Concise Encyclopedia* offers this definition of swing:

> Jazz played with a steady beat using the harmonic structure of popular songs and the blues as the basis for improvisations and arrangements. . . . Swing is characterized by syncopated rhythmic momentum with equal stress accorded to the four beats of a measure. Larger jazz bands required some arranged material, and Fletcher Henderson, Duke Ellington, and Count Basie were the primary innovators of big band swing. In smaller ensembles, improvised instrumental solos generally follow a rendering of the melody. ("Swing," Answers.com)

At the same time, the term swing is often used in a more qualitative sense to describe an ephemeral jazz quality that really "cooks" or stays "in the pocket."

Listening is an invaluable teaching tool for both the jazz and swing styles. Comparing and contrasting several different recordings of a song by different performers, while following along with a lead sheet, will help you discover that the good jazz artist respects the composer's overall intentions, even as they vary the melody and rhythms. As you learn to listen more closely, you will begin to hear the "inner time" that underlies songs in the swing and jazz styles.

Potter (2000) makes the following distinctions between swing and jazz:

> There is something fundamentally escapist about the concept of "swing," that intangible ingredient that separates off jazz musicians from other members of the human race. Swing is both of the body and of the mind: for singers it means a uniquely vibrant way of enunciating text, a way of obliquely relating syllables to underlying pulse in an almost physical way while communicating in a purely cerebral fashion with fellow musicians. . . .
> Swing is a manipulation of tempo, working between the beats. A speech like shaping of syllables, words and phrases is far more likely to facilitate it than the sustained and cultured tone of a conventional singer. (54–55)

In summary, in the jazz style, the lead sheet is a starting point from which the singer progresses to a wide variety of techniques to make the song personal and distinctive, which is the hallmark of an excellent jazz artist. Again, developing these "chops" is a great asset for music theater singers, since these jazz techniques are common stylistic characteristics found in the music theater repertoire.

Examples of musicals where the jazz style of singing is used are *City of Angels* (1989) by Coleman and Zippel; *Swing* (1999) by Taylor-Corbett; and *Jelly's Last Jam* (1992) by Morton, Henderson, and Birkenhead. Jazz belters include Etta James and Patti Austin.

ROCK STYLE AND SINGING

Rock-and-roll originated from an amalgamation of White country music, boogie-woogie, gospel, and African American rhythm and blues during the 1950s. It has since splintered into an astonishing number of subgenres (punk rock, soul, acid rock, folk rock, heavy metal, disco, et al.) and has become popular all over the world (Middleton, 2000). Because of this diversity, there is no one simple description or definition of rock music, though the *Oxford Grove Music Encyclopedia* says that rock-and-roll songs use "amplified singing and electric instruments (usually a lead electric guitar, a prominent rhythm section of bass guitar and drums, and often a rhythm guitar, and keyboard instrument), have a strong rhythmic drive intended to encourage listeners to dance, and appeal principally to young people."

Like swing, rock is more than just a musical genre. As the online Urban Dictionary explains it, "Rock and Roll . . . is a philosophy, attitude, and way of life. The purpose of Rock 'n Roll as opposed to other types of music, is to rebel" (Urbandictionary.com).

From a vocal standpoint, rock blurs the boundary between speech and singing. Distortion, variation of sounds, and heterogeneity of sounds are other common traits of rock singing. "Rock singing rests solidly on rhythm, electronic amplification, and the texture of the music and lyrics blended with the instruments backing up the vocals as a total sonic picture" (LoVetri, 2013).

Rock is characterized by straight tone production, volume (but no particular resonance), and a wide variety of registers, including falsetto and many "noise" timbres: shouts, whoops, yells, growls, grunts, screams, shrieks, humming, and wordless moans (Edwin, 2003). Word articulation varies from inarticulate (think: "Louie Louie") to very clear enunciation. Rock singing is usually loud and predominantly a highly energetic, physical form of vocal production. Because of that, rock singing is often very demanding on the voice. A sound understanding of how to accomplish these sounds without vocal injury is crucial. Sometimes a rock singer is seated to play an instrument, and the sitting position can have an adverse impact on one's singing. You need to learn how to sit in a way that allows for healthy singing, with your upper torso upright to enable deep breathing and your neck area free of tension. Even if you're standing, however, rock singing can be challenging. "A guitarist who sings is holding the instrument somewhere in front of the chest and ribs, or hips, and might also be moving around. A vocalist who is free to move may be very active while singing. All these factors matter when evaluating the functional behaviors of voice, and the restrictions or demands of live performance" (LoVetri, 2013).

Personality is another important factor in rock singing. A strong, well-defined persona, including a clear, personal style and point of view, is just as important as is a strong voice and body, since rock singing is very demanding on both (LoVetri, 2002). Despite what you do as a rock performer, though, the role of the sound engineer is often just as important as that of the singer in both the studio and live performance venues and accomplishes much of the final rock singing sound.

Examples of musicals in the rock style are *Hair* (1967) by MacDermot, Ragni, and Rado; *Tommy* (1992) by Townshend and McAnuff; *Rent* (1996) by Larson; and *Jesus Christ Superstar* (1971) by Lloyd Webber and Rice. Rock belt singers include Shirley Bassey, Cher, Celine Dion, Whitney Houston, and Bette Midler.

POP STYLE AND SINGING

The term "pop" originated in Britain in the mid-1950s to describe rock-and-roll and the many youth inventions derived from popular art and culture. The emotive and rhythmic elements of blues, the simple folk elements of country and western, and primitive jazz ideas from boogie-woogie were joined together to create the pop style (Gammond, 1991). The genre tends to feature a wide variety of tempos, from slow to bouncy; loud vocals and drums; quiet guitar(s); and often sentimental lyrics about love or love dilemmas (Gammond, 1991). The style was cultivated and developed in the United States and Britain during the ensuing decades and is now popular in one form or another in most parts of the world. The popularity of the music, and its icons such as Perry Como, Diana Ross, Madonna, Michael Jackson, and Justin Bieber, has been enhanced by the ever-changing capabilities of music technology and media outlets.

Comparing rock and pop helps define both genres. Rock is generally described as "harder," more aggressive, and more improvisatory, while pop tends to be "softer" and more "arranged" and draws more on older popular music conventions, styles, and patterns. The gray area between the two is still unclear, constantly changing, and controversial. Pop is often considered (mere) entertainment and more commercial, while rock is usually regarded as more authentic and closer to art (Middleton, 2001). Pop music is what we generally hear on the "Top 40" radio programs (About.com). "Pop music is heard on television shows like *American Idol*, *The Voice*, and the *X Factor*. The pop stars, old and new, are the singers who are most likely to be well known to the general public. The lines between styles can be very blurred, with rock and rhythm and blues holding forth as having the strongest influences" (LoVetri, 2013).

Pop singing encompasses a wide range of singers and styles and is always changing to meet current tastes (LoVetri, 2013). The pop singing style requires varying tone qualities, variable ranges, excellent pitch, no special resonance adjustment, and a speech-oriented production. Pop singers need strong dance skills, the ability to memorize music quickly, excellent arrangements, and usually youth. Pop musicals include *Grease* (1971) by Jacobs, Casey, and Calhoun; *Little Shop of Horrors* (1986) by Menken and Ashman; *Smokey Joe's Café* (1995) by Lieber; and *Godspell* (1971) by Schwartz and Tebelak.

The musicals *Tommy* (1968), *Godspell* (1971), *Jesus Christ Superstar* (1971), and *Grease* (1971) were all influenced by the fusion of pop and rock elements (Gammond, 1991), and the two genres have continued to influence each other and morph into new variations of each style. This conglomeration of style characteristics and vocal production continues to be heard in the new musicals being written for the Broadway stage. Listen to pop belters Mariah Carey, Kelly Clarkson, and Barbra Streisand.

Pop, rock, swing, folk, gospel, rhythm and blues—trying to master all these different singing styles, and then learning to mix and match them, can take years. If you want to be a successful music theater performer, though, the effort is necessary. Gone are the days when a singer could make it as a "one trick pony." The same can be said for vocal coaches.

> As long as singing teachers look for one kind of vocal behavior or one type of production, an impasse concerning contemporary commercial styles of singing will continue to exist. The many and varied technical requirements call for resourceful, creative use of vocal technique. (LoVetri, 2002, 251)

From a technical point of view, it is important for singers to remember that each of the plethora of contemporary commercial music styles requires a different configuration of source (larynx) and filter (pharynx/throat), different activities of the articulators, and different use of the breath (LoVetri, 2002).

BIBLIOGRAPHY

About.com. "Top 40/Pop." Retrieved July 4, 2013, from http://www.top40.about.com.
Answers.com. "Folk music." Retrieved July 4, 2013, from http://www.answers.com/folk-music&r=67.

Answers.com. "Swing." Retrieved July 9, 2013, from http://www.answers.com/topic/swing-music-2.

Cooper, G. (2003). Once more with feeling: The crossover artist's first steps in making an emotional connection with a popular or jazz song. *Journal of Singing, 60*(2), 153–57.

Edwin, R. (2003). A broader Broadway. *Journal of Singing, 59*(5), 431–32.

———. (January 24, 2006). Personal communication.

Gammond, P. (1991). *The Oxford companion to popular music*. New York: Oxford University Press.

Hall, K. S. (2006). Music theater vocal pedagogy and styles: An introductory teaching guide for experienced classical singing teachers. Doctoral Dissertation, Teachers College, Columbia University.

LoVetri, J. (2002). Contemporary commercial music: More than one way to use the vocal tract. *Journal of Singing, 58*(3), 249–52.

LoVetri, J. (2003). Female chest voice. *Journal of Singing, 60*(2), 161–64.

———. (2013). The necessity of using functional training in the independent studio. *Journal of Singing, 70*(1), 79–86.

Middleton, R. (2000). Rock singing. In J. Potter (Ed.), *The Cambridge companion to singing* (pp. 28–41). Cambridge: Cambridge University Press.

———. (Ed.). (2001). *The new Grove dictionary of music and musicians*. London: Macmillan Publishers Limited.

Morath, M. (2002). *Popular standards*. New York: The Berkley Publishing Group.

Peckham, A. (2003). Vocalise patterns for the contemporary singer. Journal of Singing, 59(3), 215–20.

Potter, J. (Ed). (2000). *The Cambridge companion to singing* Cambridge: Cambridge University Press.

Roll, C. (2012). Musical theater singing in the 21st century: Examining the pedagogy of the female belt voice. Unpublished advanced proposal, Teachers College, Columbia University.

Saunders-Barton, Mary. (April 5, 2006). Personal communication.

Sundberg, J. (2000). Where does the sound come from? In J. Potter (Ed.), *The Cambridge companion to singing* (pp. 231–47). Cambridge: Cambridge University Press.

Taylor, D. (2006). *Elements of gospel*. Unpublished manuscript, East Carolina University.

———. (March 10, 2006). Personal communication.

Tribe, I. M. (Ed.). (2001). *The new Grove dictionary of music and musicians*. London: Macmillan Publishers Limited.

Urban Dictionary. "Rock and Roll." Retrieved from http://www.urbandictionary.com/define.php?term=Rock%20'n%20Roll.

7

PERFORMING MUSIC THEATER

Another aspect of music theater training is learning how to work with a wide and varied assortment of professional artists: singing teachers, vocal coaches, conductors, composers, and others will greatly impact your music theater education and career. Understanding the role of each—what they do and why; what they expect, need, and require—is key to your success.

For instance, what is the difference between a singing teacher and a voice/vocal coach? They are not the same! If you are a beginner, you need to study with a singing teacher first; after you have established a strong basic singing technique, you can begin working with a coach, too. Understanding this distinction is crucial, and many young singers have no idea that there are two types of singing voice professionals or that their roles differ in your vocal development.

SINGING TEACHER

Teaching you how to physically produce your singing sound is the role of a singing teacher. One of the most important aspects to remember when choosing a singing teacher is that, while more and more singing teachers have begun to educate themselves about music theater singing, many do not have training in the specific mechanics of music theater vocal production. While there are similarities between music theater and classical singing, there are also significant differences. Many singing teachers have received only classical training and have sung only in the classical style. As a result, even though opinions and attitudes are changing, many classical teachers believe mix/belt singing is unhealthy and undesirable, even though voice science has patently proven otherwise. You want to be sure to choose a teacher who has training in music theater singing mix/belt techniques, and one who holds a favorable opinion about the genre. You also need to find out about their training and background, as well as their success rate in regard to their current music theater students.

Once you have chosen a teacher, she or he will first teach you how to develop your "head register." Once that aspect of your singing is established, healthy, and reliable, your singing teacher will introduce you to mix/belt singing techniques, which are essential in music theater. At the first lesson, she or he will evaluate your voice and determine your vocal needs, then you will be given a set of appropriate exercises to build the different aspects of your singing technique. A singing teacher can also help you determine appropriate songs for your level of vocal development.

Weekly lessons are the most common regimen when studying voice. In between the weekly lessons, you will need to practice, almost daily, the material introduced at your lessons. The amount of time you practice will increase over time. Remember, your voice is a muscle, and it needs to be gradually strengthened, just as you would build up your legs for running. Your practice sessions will mirror your voice lessons: once your vocal muscle (stamina) increases, you can practice for longer periods of time. Like any muscle, if your voice is exercised too long or incorrectly, you are defeating the purpose of practicing. Your teacher will guide you as to how much time you can practice each practice session and will build on what you accomplish during your practice sessions at your weekly lessons. Practice is where you make most of your vocal progress; a voice teacher can help you only as much as you help yourself.

One way to find singing teachers and vocal coaches is to listen to successful singers and ask them about their training. Before starting with a new teacher, you might ask to sit in on a lesson first, since observing might help you determine if that instructor is a good "fit" for you.

Voice training can begin at a very early age, preferably with private, one-on-one instruction. Private voice lessons are rarely included as part of a K–12 school curriculum, so you will need to find a private instructor or take part in group voice classes, which are often offered by community music schools, private studio teachers, and other venues. If you decide to major in music theater and earn a BFA in college, you will be required to take private (applied) weekly voice lessons. Private weekly coaching sessions are sometimes provided, too.

The last, and perhaps most important, key to becoming a successful voice student is to develop good habits. To get maximum benefit from your lessons, I encourage you to practice regularly, be on time for your lessons, ask questions, be positive, take care of your whole health, and show respect for your teachers at all times.

VOCAL COACH/ACCOMPANIST

A coach will teach you the characteristics of each vocal style (pop, rock, jazz, etc.), ensure that the pitches and rhythms of the vocal line are learned correctly, and help you learn to sing your part with piano accompaniment. A coach can also help you choose songs in the appropriate key for your voice and help select the strongest sixteen- to thirty-two-bar song cuts to use for your auditions. Your audition book needs to contain both up-tempo and ballad selections representing each music theater style. Another important role a coach plays is to help you choose audition material appropriate for your voice and physical type (more on auditioning and physical typing later). The music in your audition book should be clearly marked with cuts, page turns, and breath marks and should be legible. Be sure your music is secured in a three-ring binder with easy page turns. Placing your music inside plastic sheets often causes glare, and this makes it difficult for your coach/accompanist to easily read what they need to play. New York City coach Robert Marks presents music theater audition workshops and recommends that your audition book contain the following selections. He adds that all songs need to be marked for sixteen-bar cuts, occasionally thirty-two-bar cuts, and even eight-bar cuts (R. Marks, e-mail communication, June 28, 2013).

- Traditional (Golden Age) Broadway (both ballad and up-tempo)
- Character piece (funny)
- Contemporary Broadway (both ballad and up-tempo)
- Simple accompaniment (even a bad pianist can get through it)
- Simple vocal (you can do it even if not at your best)

- Something special you do well in the following styles: jazz, Sond-heim, country, classical, pop
- 1950s–1960s song (for *Hairspray*, *Grease*, or some jukebox musi-cals)
- Non-Broadway pop/rock

Although a voice coach will not, for the most part, instruct you on vocal production (how you produce the sounds you sing), there is some overlap between the roles of the voice coach and singing teacher. For instance, coaches generally do not work on vocal technique with you, but if you need to sing a particular word or phrase in "chest register" and you are not doing that, a coach might ask you to make that vocal adjustment.

Voice coach and pianist professor Daniel Lockert, who coaches music theater voice majors and also teaches collaborative piano arts at Notre Dame de Namur University in Belmont, California, provides an example of the necessary overlap between a vocal coach and singing teacher: "Music theater singers need to be reminded where to breathe! They separate the music from the spoken words when they should be connecting them. Working on their songs as monologues can help them understand where to breathe" (D. Lockert, telephone communication, June 22, 2013). So while a voice teacher will teach you healthy breathing and support technique for singing, a vocal coach's job is to help you learn to apply that knowledge, for example, remind you to breathe in the appropriate places in the music.

You will work with many coaches and teachers throughout your ca-reer, and no two instructors will teach you in the same way. You have to be flexible and ready to adapt to their vocabulary and style of teaching or coaching.

There is no substitute for in-person instruction; *watching* someone else learn isn't the same as hands-on learning. In this regard, Lockert has noticed a disturbing trend in young theater students: "They listen to You-Tube performances and copy vocal mannerisms, phrasing ideas, etc. That is not a good thing" (D. Lockert, telephone communication, June 22, 2013). He goes on to cite the recent *American Idol* incident involving Harry Connick Jr., when Connick was asked to coach a "standard" piece with each contestant. At the individual coaching sessions, Connick criti-cized the young contestants for having no point of reference or under-standing of the historical context of their songs. He told them they needed to know the original melody of what they were singing, and they needed to respect the lyrics by understanding their meaning. "They really need to know the original song, what the words mean," says Lockert. "They need to look up who the lyricist is, who the composer is. The thread of the historical timeline is so important. What I've discovered is that young college students have no point of reference about our fantastic history of music theater" (D. Lockert, telephone communication, June 22, 2013).

Another acting teacher, who teaches music theater performance to students all the way from kindergarten through college, echoes that opinion. She says there are a lot of young people coming up who are good singers, but the biggest problem she encounters is their complete lack of understanding of what they're saying/singing. When they just speak the lyrics, they often can't remember them, she says, because "they're completely disconnected from them and their meaning" (J. Dellger, e-mail communication, June 30, 2013). One way to overcome that, she advises, is to speak the lyrics as a poem or monologue. The same teacher encounters a lot of music theater students "over-singing" in a pop style. She adds, "They're copying *American Idol* rather than finding their truth in the lyrics and music" (J. Dellger, e-mail communication, June 30, 2013).

At Notre Dame de Namur University in Belmont, California, Lockert is developing a timeline thread in his music and theater classes to facilitate teaching music theater students the importance of connecting all the elements of a music theater performance. "A twenty-year-old won't naturally gravitate toward connecting music history issues," he says. "We must find a way to teach them this issue" (D. Lockert, telephone communication, June 22, 2013).

It is important to know and understand how all the great music theater composers are connected and how they wrote for singers. For instance, sometimes music is to be performed exactly as notated on the page, while at other times the vocal line is expected to be "taken off the page." This means that a singer must first study what the composer wrote (the notes, rhythms, and words) on the music staff. After the written vocal line is learned (internalized), the phrases can then be sung with a more conversational rhythm and phrasing, commonly referred to as "back phrasing." Lockert points out that some composers expect and want their music to be "taken off the page," while others do not. For example, Stephen Sondheim and Robert Jason Brown want their compositions sung precisely as written (D. Lockert, telephone communication, June 22, 2013). Many other contemporary composers, especially the rock and pop style composers, do not, and to do so would not be stylistically appropriate.

Dr. Beverly Patton, conductor, coach, and voice teacher at Penn State University, says that in previous generations educators advised singers away from listening to recordings. Now, however, YouTube and other online sources are a great place to listen and learn about the various styles found in music theater singing. "Listen to at least four recordings; figure out what works and what doesn't. It's a great learning tool for understanding styles" (B. Patton, telephone communication, June 30, 2013). Note that Dr. Patton encourages singers to listen to recordings to understand style, not to copy another artist's style.

A word of caution: With the ever-increasing availability and use of the public domain for performance purposes, you need to develop a healthy respect for the intellectual property rights of your coach or teacher. As one coach says, "I have to explain to students, 'Do not put videos of our coaching sessions on YouTube without my permission!'" He goes on to add that, in this day and age, there is a different mentality because the Internet is part of their daily lives, something that didn't exist in previous generations. "They don't question putting whatever they want into the public domain. But they need to learn how to be discriminating about what they post, and that they must get permission from the pianist, coach, or teacher to post publically" (D. Lockert, telephone communication, June 22, 2013).

MUSICIANSHIP SKILLS

In addition to vocal technique and application, voice students would be well served to develop professional-caliber musicianship, especially a working knowledge of music theory and sight-reading. Often coaches cite poor musicianship skills as one of the biggest challenges they face when working with music theater singers. "They are lacking 'cracker jack musicianship,' but need it," reports Dr. Patton. The problem is that music theater students are being trained in many different areas at once, and musicianship training tends to be rushed or shortchanged. Those with piano skills move ahead more easily, while others lacking such training will be forced to play catch-up. Musicianship is a must, though, as the demands of the professional world simply do not allow a young singer to learn those music skills on the job. As a conductor, Dr. Patton says, "I want the best musicians I can get because I have to work so fast" (B. Patton, June 30, 2013, telephone communication).

Joe Dellger, a highly accomplished music theater actor with a beautiful and versatile baritone voice, agrees on the importance of musicianship skills.

> My first impulse is to say that performers need to learn to sight read well. This skill will come in handy, not just when learning music for auditions quickly—which will often be necessary—but, most importantly, once they've booked the gig and are sitting in a room full of good people who can sight read. Every music director will love the singer who can move through the music quickly, the actor they can trust to do what's been taught the next time they go through the material. I just did a reading of a new show, and I run into that a lot. I really wish I'd learned that skill better when I was younger, because it seems to have gotten increasingly rusty over time. (J. Dellger, e-mail communication, June 30, 2013)

"They need sight reading skills," says coach and pianist Lockert. "You also need to know the piano part and interplay between the piano and voice. In other words, sing exactly what's on the page *first!*" (D. Lockert, June 22, 2013, telephone communication).

Nine times out of ten, Lockert finds, music theater students don't have the background and musicianship skills they need: "Sight reading is a huge thing. They have to learn to read music." This is not a simple task. Rather than trying to learn everything at once, though, as young singers are wont to do, the most effective way to learn a song is by first learning the components separately, says Lockert. This approach allows you to focus more clearly on each aspect of the learning process, which results in learning the song correctly. Learn the notes and rhythms, he advises. Sing the pitches on a vowel, and speak the words in rhythm. The latter technique is called "monologuing." "Theater students are used to monologuing," says Lockert. "It's very important to monologue a song" (D. Lockert, telephone communication, June 22, 2013).

Breaking down the components also allows you to stay focused on your singing technique, how you are producing your sound. Often when a singer tries to learn everything at once, they forget to sing with optimal technique because other aspects of learning distract them. Consequently, ineffective, rather than healthy, habits are developed and reinforced (D. Lockert, telephone communication, June 22, 2013).

"Many singers read music less well than instrumentalists, and some read not at all," conductor and coach Mort Stine says. To alleviate the problem, he urges conductors and coaches to be patient and flexible. "Never feel you have the right to embarrass or punish them," he says. "Your only valid choice is patience and respect for their ability to make a beautiful and expressive sound." Another solution for choral numbers—which Stine admits "may horrify some purists"—is to give singers a choice in which note they sing: "If a choral number ends with a big loud chord, it's often fun to let the chorus 'fake' the last chord—to sing the note they would prefer to sing, as long as it's 'in the chord.' Also, it's usually in their best range, though you may have to adjust the balance sometimes" (M. Stine, e-mail communication, June 25, 2013).

COLLEGIATE MUSICIANSHIP TEACHING MODEL FOR MUSIC THEATER STUDENTS

Since the musicianship skills requirement of music theater students is different in many ways from the classical model, many university theater departments have begun teaching these skills differently in order to meet those specific needs. For example, at one university they have a course nicknamed "gorilla piano skills for music theater majors." The course assumes some working knowledge of music reading, and the students sight read actual music theater repertoire—a task they will be called on to do regularly during their careers.

During the summer of 2013, a group of music theater students from that same university took part in a twenty-nine-hour Equity workshop reading of *The Stardust Road*, a new musical review for the Hoagy Carmichael estate. At the conclusion of the workshop, the music director wrote a letter to the university faculty

> I wanted to express my specific satisfaction, bordering on amazement, with the group of actors you assembled for our presentation. Without exception, they were actors with music skills of the highest order. The fact that they were as accomplished and willing to learn whatever was put in front of them, and do it well, allowed me the rare opportunity of creating without concern of limitations. This allowed me to more fully

realize some of the arrangement ideas in my mind (that were, in turn, likely inspired by the specific personnel at my disposal). I cannot overstate the ease of working with a group of actors who were all adept at the skill of reading music. They were also quick and attentive to making "fixes" that were a natural result of the rehearsal process. As you well know, a sharp pencil and the ability to use it are greatly appreciated within the time constraints of a twenty-nine hour reading. I certainly don't mean to imply that these abilities are nonexistent in the world but it is rare to come into an entire room of equally prepared, enthusiastic, and talented performers to work with. They were incredibly focused, consistent and, to top it off, a lovely bunch of people; I would work with any one of them again in a heartbeat. (L. Yurman, August 14, 2013, e-mail communication)

This letter demonstrates that while music theater singers can find success without music reading skills, the chances of finding work in a very competitive field are greatly enhanced by taking the time to develop strong music reading skills.

ACTING TEACHERS AND DIRECTORS

As part of your music theater training, you will be taking acting classes. There are many approaches and techniques to acting, but one of the most useful for the music theater student is to take at least one class that combines acting with singing, where a pianist is provided so you can sing and perform songs from different eras for an acting teacher. Often these types of classes are called "techniques classes." Your technique needs to become habitual so that you can adjust your voice in whatever ways the acting teacher requests. Vocal technique is learned in the voice studio, but vocal "function" is a broader term that refers to all the vocal adjustments a singer must make to respond to the needs of the director, explains Dr. Patton (B. Patton, telephone communication, June 30, 2013).

DANCE TEACHERS

Since dance and movement are such integral parts of performing music theater, learning to dance—or at least move well—is essential. Music theater artists are often described as the quintessential "triple threat" performers, meaning you must be able to act, sing, and dance well. The earlier that dance skills are acquired, the better, and training needs to include a sound foundation in all dance styles. Jazz and tap dance are part of many music theater shows, but there are many other ways to dance and move. The more versatile you are as a performer, the more castable you will become. Some shows have specialized roles that call for ballet, for example, while others might require the actor to do some folk, Renaissance, modern, or character dancing. The better you can move, the broader your horizons. You couldn't effectively play Puck, for instance, if you didn't have some training in mime and gymnastics. You couldn't do slapstick if you couldn't take a pratfall. And you couldn't perform certain Shakespeare parts if you couldn't do stage fighting.

That is the key: As a stage performer, you are more than just a voice, a face, and some dance steps. You are a whole being, and you need to be able to communicate effectively with your entire body. That is why it is extremely helpful to take as many kinds of movement and dance classes as possible. Private and community dance programs are offered in most cities and towns in the United States, so start taking advantage of as many types of dance and movement training as soon as possible, and continue your training throughout your career. You'll move better, look better, feel better, perform better, and greatly enhance your music theater career.

CONDUCTORS AND COMPOSERS

When you work with a conductor, just as with an acting teacher, it is important to remember and understand the difference between technique and function. Vocal function is a result of and dependent upon a strong singing technique: you use your technical skills to produce the desired function requested by either a conductor or director. Function comes into play during rehearsals, how a singer responds to vocal and/or acting adjustments requested by a conductor or director. A conductor may ask you for a certain style or sound, and you need to be able to respond to that request. In order to functionally achieve what a conductor or director asks, your technique must be highly developed and reliable. Conductors must focus mostly on the orchestra, not on whether a singer can or cannot do something. That is your job.

Some things are beyond your control, though. Dr. Patton states that often music theater composers do not understand how to write for the singing voice. Young composers, especially, often do not have enough knowledge of the voice, and they are unwittingly writing overly difficult music. For example, she points out, "Pop singers don't sing eight shows a week, but music theater composers often want music theater performers to create that pop sound." As a result, singers are being asked to perform in a style that cannot be sustained long term (B. Patton, telephone communication, June 30, 2013).

What is the solution to this emerging problem? First of all, composers need to attend voice lessons, listen, and learn more about the voice. Music directors would benefit from playing for voice lessons. Also, transposing the music can help a great deal when a song is written or orchestrated in a key that is inappropriate for the singer in question. This presents its own dilemma, however. "Do you honor the conductor, the composer, the arranger, or do you change the orchestration to suit the singers' voices?" asks Dr. Patton (B. Patton, June 30, 2013, telephone communication).

Orchestration is another variable. If the song is already orchestrated, do you take into consideration the singers you are working with? While this may rankle composers or music directors, changing the orchestration by reducing or lightening the texture can aid singers tremendously. To help singers adapt to the complexities of orchestration, Dr. Patton recommends playing the vocal line on the piano until the singers are sure of their part, then replacing the piano with the orchestration. "Unless they are trained musicians, you have to tell them to listen to the orchestration for their pitch. The clarinet may be playing what they are used to hearing on the piano, but the piano isn't there anymore" (B. Patton, June 30, 2013, telephone communication).

Lockert comments on a problematic new genre or phenomenon he's encountered where hip, modern composers are "not writing for the Broadway stage, but for the underground, i.e., 'a Greenwich Village Club somewhere.'" He describes this music as wordy, full of expletives ("****this, **** that"), with little harmonic progression (use of only two chords is not unusual) and the portrayal of banal subject matters (e.g., shopping). He believes it is important to tactfully advise young singers about the phenomenon. Don't say the songs are awful, though, he recommends; instead, expose them to higher-quality music and lyrics of substance (D. Lockert, June 22, 2013, telephone communication).

Lawrence Goldberg, a widely accomplished music theater conductor, generously offers advice for music theater performers from his perspective as one of today's leading Broadway conductors (*The Drowsy Chaperone*, *The Producers*, *Thoroughly Modern Millie*, and, most recently, the national tour of *South Pacific*). He calls his advice "Ten Things Aspiring Music Theater Singers Need to Know" (L. Goldberg, e-mail communication, July 15, 2013).

Music theater is a dramatic art.

This is the number one thing to keep in mind and strongly influences the other nine tips. Singers are often primarily musicians, rather than actors, but Broadway singing must be guided more strongly by dramatic parameters than by musical ones. Of course, vocal technique and musicianship are very important, but they must be used as tools to serve the overarching dramatic needs. Choices of phrasing, vocal placement, tempo, strictness of rhythm, dynamics, and so on, may be perfectly valid considerations from a musical standpoint, but if they conflict with the character or the dramatic context, then they are not necessarily the right choices.

You need a broad spectrum of skills.

Musicians become used to the notion that honing one specific skill as close as possible to perfection will lead to success. Music theater, however, is a multiskill environment. The strongest singers in the world will not find success if they cannot also adequately act or dance, or preferably both. Aspiring music theater singers who already have strong vocal skills are better served putting more effort into learning to act and/or dance, rather than continuing to "perfect" their singing voice. This is not to take away from the importance of maintaining a strong and versatile singing technique—it is just a reminder that better acting will improve a singing audition more than will marginally better or "more perfect" singing (assuming one already has professional-quality singing technique). "I have seen many marginal singers who are strong actors win singing roles over far better singers who do not have the acting skills," says Goldberg.

Musical versatility is very helpful.

Music theater embraces many different musical and vocal styles. Not everyone can be equally good at them all, so it's best to know what style you're most suited for and pursue shows and roles that showcase that style. Having said that, it's always helpful to increase your knowledge and experience by singing in other styles to maximize your versatility. Often actor/singers are required to "play against type" for comic or dramatic reasons, so the more comfortable and versatile you are in as many different styles as possible, the more hirable you will be.

Musical literacy is very helpful, but not a prerequisite.

Singers always help themselves by being more musically literate—that is, being able to read and sight sing printed music, to follow and understand musical direction and accompaniments, to recognize harmonic chord types and progressions, to comprehend standard Italian musical terminology, and so on. These skills make learning new music much easier and faster, but they generally will not help you get work other than readings. I'm constantly working with successful actor/singers who are musically completely illiterate, other than being able to see that notes go up or down. These people continue to work steadily because they are very strong actors who can sing "well enough," and who have the ability to learn music by rote.

Singers must analyze, understand, and convey the text.

Too many singers clearly do not understand the importance of the text. They're so consumed by the vocal and musical elements that they forget that the text is the predominant language of dramatic communication, not just sounds to vocalize on. Beyond merely advancing the story line, the whole reason for a song in a musical is that a character must express a strong emotion or idea. Yes, both the music and vocal melody participate crucially to that end (and yes, there are times when writers intentionally eschew words or comprehensibility), but for the vast majority of songs, the words supply most of the emotional and intellectual context and content, and must be the starting point for the singer's understanding of the song.

In other words, a singer must understand *what* is being said, *why* the character is choosing to say it, and *how* the character feels or thinks about what he or she is saying. He or she must also take into account any potential thoughts or feelings that are *not said* that may be part of his inner monologue. This is all part of a dramatic analysis of the text. The singer should also analyze the craft of the lyric—the implicit rhythm of the words, the rhyme scheme (including less obvious inner rhymes), how brittle or supple the words sound, and so forth—and how that relates to the dramatic content. Think of the vast differences in the crafting of songs between, say, "Oklahoma" and "A Little Night Music"; a thorough understanding of the mechanical particulars of those songs will help you look below the obvious surface contrasts to see how and why the characters in those two shows are so very different from each other.

Once a lyric is fully analyzed and understood in dramatic context, then the singer can pair it back with the music, and often find deeper ways that the music supports or informs the text, leading to a richer and more deeply felt performance.

Finally, the singer must remember that the text must be intelligible to the listener if the writer's intention is to be fully realized. The act of singing can often obfuscate the clarity of words, especially in higher registers. Voice teachers often concentrate on vowel sounds, since that's where the vocal resonance lies; but the singer must remember that consonants are more important for intelligibility and that they often must be overarticulated in order to be conveyed clearly. Vowels can be thought of as the river, and consonants as the riverbank: it is the harder consonants that contain and help define the softer vowel sounds. The listener cannot ride the journey of the song if she or he is struggling to make out the words. As Goldberg says, "I particularly appreciate singers who 'make a meal of the words.'"

Acting is about thoughts/emotions that lead to utterance.

"I can't teach acting in one paragraph of advice, but I can help illuminate a concept that most singers fail to realize," says Goldberg. "Acting is not about what someone is feeling or doing *while* they are speaking or singing a text; rather, it is about the thoughts or feelings or actions that *lead* them to say or sing the text." A big part of the text analysis needs to be figuring out what those motivational keys are for the character and incorporating them into the performance of the song so that it appears that the character is responding to the inner impulse that caused him or her to utter those words. More often than not, these words are supposed to spring spontaneously from the character in the context of the situational moment, yet singers often deliver lyrics in a way that sounds too much like the prewritten text that they are. Of course, the *singer* must know the text ahead of singing it, but most often the *character* should not, until the motivational thought triggers it. Being able to convincingly embody the cause/effect relationship of thoughts/feelings to words is what makes good acting in a song. The great actor/singers always make it look and sound like they are making it up on the spot.

Be careful of back phrasing.

These days, too many singers automatically back phrase anything with emotional content—often as a poor, lazy substitute for more specific acting. Back phrasing has its valid and powerful uses, often to convey a character's emotional difficulty with the text or a moment when she or he must think of how to express a thought. The musical tension that back phrasing creates can often heighten a climactic phrase in a song. However, the singer should bear in mind that back phrasing often bears diminishing returns: the more you back phrase in a song, the less effective it is.

"As a conductor, I hate it when I feel like I'm dragging a singer through a song, as if they're reluctant to sing it," says Goldberg. A song ought to spring forth from a character because she or he feels an urgency to express a strong thought or emotion. The character should *drive* the song and compel the music to be formed and follow along. It is not the music that should motivate the character to sing but quite the other way around. There is great power to be harnessed by the singer singing the written rhythms on time and trusting the composer's choices.

Be intelligent about strictness of pitch and rhythm.

This is somewhat related to back phrasing, but a separate issue. Music uses a precise notational system of pitch and rhythm, but often too much precision can be detrimental to a performance. Though we usually want the singer to sing "in tune," overly precise pitch precludes the dramatic use of inflection. Similarly, if rhythms are too strictly adhered to, words may come over as too stilted.

As in most music, a humanizing element needs to be applied, especially in music theater singing, which is all about the human element. A good composer will strive to set lyrics in a rhythm that allows the words to retain a measure of their natural spoken rhythm, except when a specific dramatic or comic effect is being sought. A singer should take an intelligent approach to determining how strictly to interpret the musical writing. Much of the time, rhythms can be somewhat relaxed to sound more natural and communicative. Like back phrasing, however, changing the rhythm should not be done mindlessly, and care should be taken not to alter the composer's intent. For instance, sometimes a more precise, stilted delivery is intended to heighten comedy, or a specific rhythm might be an important motivic element to the song that should not be changed.

Most music theater composers write in rather simple rhythms, and they have always expected singers to automatically make the rhythms sound natural. However, some more sophisticated composers (Leonard Bernstein, Stephen Sondheim, Stephen Schwartz, Jason Robert Brown) tend to write more exactly what they mean, even to the extent of writing out the back phrasing they want. Generally, the more complicated the rhythm appears, the more strictly the composer intends for it to be adhered to, but the singer should always balance that intelligently with the dramatic needs of the character.

Be a team player with your accompanist.

Whether you're singing with just piano accompaniment or being supported by a conductor with a pit or concert orchestra, you should recognize your role in collaborating with the musicians. Accompaniment does not happen magically, though many singers behave as though it does. A good conductor or pianist will breathe with the singer and anticipate phrasing choices in support of the singer. A good singer should reciprocate by helping the accompanist or conductor to anticipate what's coming. The best singers almost conduct the song themselves by use of their breath and body language.

Rules are meant to be broken!

"There are undoubtedly exceptions to every item on this list. As in any art, there is no such thing as perfection, and often better art is achieved by the judicious, conscious breaking of some rules. In music theater singing (except perhaps in revue-style shows—there's your exception!), my number one rule ought to be the prevailing guide: *music theater is a dramatic art*," Goldberg reminds us. "Any other rule can be broken if it is justified by dramatic circumstances. Your performance as a music theater singer is enhanced by your singularity, your individualism, and your unique approach that differs from everyone else's. Discover how a song works for you, and *own* it. If it's dramatically compelling enough, it will be memorable and successful!" (L. Goldberg, e-mail communication, July 15, 2013).

MICROPHONES/AMPLIFICATION

In most instances when you are performing in music theater shows, your voice will be electronically amplified. Using a microphone doesn't—and shouldn't—change the way you sing. You still need to develop your full potential of sound, since a microphone and sound engineer can only work with what you give them. Sound engineers, who determine the final singing product, cannot make your voice into something it is not. If you sing poorly, your amplified voice will only be a louder version of the poor singing. Conductors have a monitor, so they can hear sounds, but they don't hear exactly what the audience is hearing because the sound engineer controls the final mix. As Dr. Patton explains, "The conductors work the ensemble acoustically, and hope that's what is being electronically amplified." She adds that music theater conductors are more and more beholden to the electronic world (B. Patton, telephone communication, June 30, 2013). So are singers, I might add!

AUDITIONING

Before you can get up there on the stage, though, you need to win the part. Auditioning is at the heart of a career in music theater, since auditions determine whether or not you will be cast in a particular show. Learning to audition well is essential to your success.

Following is some sage advice about successful auditioning from renowned New York City coach and accompanist Robert Marks (R. Marks, e-mail communication, June 28, 2013).

1. If you've planned what to sing from your own repertoire, avoid changing songs at the last minute without good reason. It's natural to second-guess yourself when under pressure, but it's probably just your nerves talking. It's always better to avoid making important decisions when under the influence of adrenaline!

2. Trying to get through your entire song when asked for only sixteen bars shows that you don't know how to follow directions. However, since a bar is not a measure of time, requesting a certain number of bars of a song is a somewhat imprecise measure. Remember that sixteen-bar auditions are essentially typecasting to determine whether you will go on to the next step of the audition process. When cutting your song, keep in mind that the requested sixteen bars should equal about thirty to forty-five seconds of singing that shows you off at your best. If the casting director is being literal about the number of bars you're permitted to sing, you'll have to be ready for that contingency with appropriate song cuts.

3. Know what you're singing about, and to whom you're singing, as well as the meaning of every single word of the lyric. "I recommend singing to one or more imaginary people, and optionally including the actual people behind the table," says Marks. When singing, don't worry too much about your hands; motion is generated by emotion, and your physical movement should evolve from your subtext.

4. Think of the waiting room as a professional workspace, and try not to let others distract you from your impending audition. Make every effort to put aside any preconceived notions about what will happen, since things constantly change in the audition room.

5. Avoid learning a new song for an audition unless required, and try not to audition with any song if you have doubts about your ability to sing it well. Worrying about hitting an uncomfortably high note, for example, may distract you throughout your performance. And don't bring any song into an audition room if it's not memorized

and prepared, since auditioners have a tendency to thumb through your book while you sing.

6. Help your accompanist help you. Never snap or clap tempo to the accompanist; give the tempo of your song by softly singing a bar or two. Mark your music carefully; if the accompanist is unable to decipher markings on music or has multiple page turns, your audition may be sabotaged. The most important thing to indicate in music cuts is what you want the accompanist to play for your introduction. The more care you take in the presentation of your audition music, the more care the accompanist will give it.

7. Increase your repertoire to include more songs in more styles, so you are ready with widely appropriate audition material.

8. It's best to avoid "signature" songs that make us think of the original artists. If you sing "Don't Rain on My Parade," it will be difficult for the casting directors not to think of Barbra Streisand or Lea Michele.

9. It's generally a good idea not to sing a song from the show you're auditioning for unless specifically requested. Why? There's no need to limit yourself to only that one role. And you don't want to appear locked into a specific performance style that might not match the director's vision of how that song should be done.

10. Remember that, no matter what, there's always the next audition. In this business, the only way to fail is to give up.

Directors will expect singer/actors to prepare a variety of acting scenes. The demands of learning all that material can be daunting, as casting agents often send so much material that actors don't have time to prepare adequately. "This is a growing source of frustration and anger in the acting community," laments one seasoned New York City music theater actor/singer. The issue, he explains, is that, "in almost no cases, will the actor be asked to read all the scenes she or he has been given to prepare, and you don't know which ones they'll ask for. The amount of time and money spent on coaching that is purely wasted on preparing material that everyone knows won't ever be presented is maddening." In addition, there is often music to learn from the show, usually more than one song. Sight reading helps, but nowadays singers also can access recordings of the accompaniment and melody for each song. This has been a tremendous help, especially for singers whose sight-reading skills aren't what they should be.

Veteran music theater actor/singer Dellger's auditioning tips include keeping songs short because it only takes a few seconds to know if someone has a voice—or more particularly, if their voice is right for the role they're casting. "Money notes," if the role requires them, are a necessary evil, so include them in the song cut you choose for your audition. As for length, "I think a one-minute song is just fine," says Dellger. "If they want to hear more, they'll ask" (J. Dellger, e-mail communication, June 30, 2013).

Another important aspect of auditioning is learning to control the audition, says Dellger. "One of the things I continue to try to get command of is controlling one's audition. This is very difficult, because there are many elements you won't be aware of until you walk in the room." He cites several examples of those unknowns that can throw an audition sideways:

1. The skill level of the accompanist ("They've ruined more than one audition for me, and paying someone to come play is expensive.");
2. The mood of the people sitting behind the audition table;
3. The quality of the reader;
4. Responding to "on the spot" acting instructions from the director;
5. Being asked, "What else do you have to sing?"
6. Being told, "Do it again this way";
7. Getting stopped and asked to start again.

How does Dellger deal with these surprise factors? "Sometimes I've said, 'If it's all right with you, I'd like to do this scene or that scene.'" Then he does the ones he feels best about. Auditioning is about much more than just your voice. You have to juggle all these factors while trying to be (or at least look) relaxed, in a good mood, and funny (that is way more important than people think). Helping them to have fun during your audition is always a good idea. If you don't believe that, try sitting outside an audition room where you can hear them all howling with laughter inside. Even if you're not their pick, making their long day a little fun is always appreciated and often memorable—which is what you want. Obviously, auditioning for a drama will temper the humor aspect. Again, you have to feel all these issues out when you walk into the audition room, though doing all this spontaneously is not an easy thing to pull off (J. Dellger, e-mail communication, June 30, 2013).

MUSIC THEATER CASTING TYPES

Physical typing is an important component to consider when choosing your repertoire. Even though a song may "fit" vocally, if you do not fit the physical and personality type required for the role, you will not get the job. The American music theater system categorizes singers by physical appearance and personality traits. Listed below are the major physical types found in music theater and one example role of each type (Michael Tahaney, personal communication, April 10, 2006; Hall, 2006):

- Historic style leading lady: Marian in *The Music Man*
- Mature leading lady (mother): Vi in *Footloose*
- Contemporary/pop leading lady: Jo in *Little Women*
- Historic style leading man: Tommy in *Brigadoon*
- Mature leading man (father): King in *The King and I*
- Contemporary/pop leading man: Danny in *Grease*
- Young female ingénue (girl next door): Louisa in *The Fantastiks*
- Sexy vamp: Rose in *Bye Bye Birdie*
- Sexy vamp that dances well: Gladys in *The Pajama Game*
- Female dance lead: Charity in *Sweet Charity*
- Young male ingénue (boy next door): Freddy in *My Fair Lady*
- Song and dance man (male dance lead or supporting): Bernardo in *West Side Story*
- Comic character type (male or female): Sancho in *Man of La Mancha*, Adelaide in *Guys and Dolls*
- Comic character that dances well: Will Parker in *Oklahoma!*
- Hipster/Rocker (male or female): Mary Magdalene in *Jesus Christ Superstar*

This chapter has given you a brief introduction to the complex and multifaceted art form of music theater. Music theater training demands multiple skills that are performed simultaneously at a high level of mastery. Talent, drive, hard work, and a large dose of good luck are key ingredients to your success in addition to a path of lifelong learning.

BIBLIOGRAPHY

Dellger, J. (2013, June 30). E-mail interview.

Goldberg, L. (2013, July 15). E-mail interview.

Hall, K. S. (2006). Music theater vocal pedagogy and styles: An introductory teaching guide for experienced classical singing teachers. Doctoral Dissertation, Teachers College, Columbia University.

Lockert, D. (2013, June 22). Telephone interview.

Marks, R. (2013, June 28). E-mail interview.

Patton, B. (2013, June 30). Telephone interview.

Stine, M. (June 25, 2013). E-mail communication.

Tahaney, M. (April 10, 2006). Personal communication.

Yurman, L. (2013, August 14). E-mail interview.

GLOSSARY

Abduction	When the vocal folds move apart and separate.
Adduction	When the vocal folds come together or approximate.
Alveoli	Tiny air sacs inside the lungs where the exchange of oxygen and carbon dioxide takes place.
Aphonia	The absence of vocal fold vibration and term commonly used when someone "loses their voice."
Arytenoid cartilages	Paired, ladle-shaped cartilages to which the vocal cords are attached.
Back phrasing	When a singer intentionally sings off tempo by singing before or after the written beat.
Ballad	A term used in the music theater that describes a song that is characterized by a slower tempo. Most music theater auditions require singers to come prepared with sixteen bars of a ballad and sixteen bars of an "up-tempo" (described below) song to demonstrate vocal and stylistic contrast. The term *ballad* can be thought of as a term that replaces art song or aria in classical singing. All styles of music theater repertoire that employ a slow tempo are called a ballad. There is no distinction in genre or style as is found in classical singing.

Ballad opera   Any British stage production from 1728 to 1760 that combines a comic or sentimental play with musical numbers that reused common tunes.

Bending   Deliberately singing above or below the pitch as an expressive device.

Bossa Nova   A style of Brazilian music invented in the late 1950s by a group of middle-class students and musicians living in the Copacabana and Ipanema beachside districts of Rio de Janeiro. The name could be translated as "the new beat" or "the new way."

Boyle's Law   In a soft-walled enclosure and at a constant temperature, pressure and volume are inversely related.

Burlesque   A musical work intended to cause laughter by caricaturing the manner or spirit of serious works.

Burletta   In England the term began to be used, in contrast to *burlesque*, for works that satirized opera but without using musical parody. Burlettas in English began to appear in the 1760s.

Character voice   A type of singing used in music theater to alter one's voice to communicate the perceived personality of the character portrayed. Most character voices are comic roles. The vocal quality is chosen to emulate the character and is expressed in an exaggerated fashion. Male and female character voice roles are found in the music theater.

Chest mix   Singing that is not pure chest register production. The chest register dominates but a small amount of head register is also present. It differs from classical singing in that the amount of chest voice used at any pitch level is more significant than in classical production.

Chest register   Singing produced primarily by the thyroarytenoid muscles of the larynx, also sometimes called chest resonance. It is also described as a sound employing heavy registration with excessive resonance in the lower formants. Some music theater voice teachers include chest voice in their definition of the belt voice, while others do not. The use of these muscles in music theater singing is still being debated. Chest register is used with more regularity and at higher pitches in music theater singing than in classical singing.

Chiaroscuro   A term derived from art. When applied to singing, it refers to a balance of high and low resonance in the voice.

Closed quotient (CQ)   The percentage of the glottal cycle in which airflow is prevented by the closure of the vocal folds.

Comic opera   A sung dramatic work of a light or comic nature, usually with a happy ending.

Commedia dell'arte   A form of improvisational theater that began in Italy in the sixteenth century, remained highly popular through the eighteenth century, and is still performed. Performances are unscripted, held outside, and employ few props.

Contemporary commercial music (CCM)   A generic descriptor developed to describe all types of nonclassical singing. CCM styles are cabaret, country, experimental, folk, gospel, jazz, music theater, pop, rock, and rhythm and blues. This term was developed to call CCM styles by what they are rather than what they are not—nonclassical.

Cricoid cartilage   A solid ring of cartilage located below and behind the thyroid cartilage.

Cricothyroid muscle   A set of paired intrinsic laryngeal muscles that are used primarily to control and assist the folds to vibrate by stretching them. The sound produced by the cricothyroid is commonly referred to as "head" register. In the classical female voice, the use of head register dominates each pitch; while in the music theater female voice, most singing is thyroarytenoid dominant. The cricothyroid muscle

	also controls pitch and consequently is used in all vocal production.
Elastic recoil pressure	The alveolar pressure derived from extended (strained) tissue in the lungs, rib cage, and the entire thorax after inspiration.
Epiglottis	The cartilage that covers over the larynx during swallowing.
Extravaganza	A literary or musical work marked by extreme freedom of style and structure and usually by elements of burlesque or parody.
Falsetto	High, light register, applied primarily to men's voices singing in the soprano or alto range.
Fantasy	A type of musical commonly set in a fantastical world and usually aimed at both children and adults.
Flamenco	A form of Spanish folk music and dance from the region of Andalusia in southern Spain. It includes singing, guitar playing, dance, and handclaps.
Formant	A resonance of the vocal tract. Formants are sound potential rather than actual sound or a result of vibrating vocal folds. Each sung vowel shapes the vocal tract differently. The different vowel shapes determine the resonance/formant. The vocal tract produces several formants. The formants are labeled as F1, F2, and so on from the lowest to the highest.
F1 and F2	The two formants that determine vowel sounds.
F3, F4, and F5	The three formants that determine vocal timbre.
Formant tuning	A boosting of intensity when F0 or one of its harmonics coincides exactly with a formant frequency. Vowels are modified during formant tuning to create maximum acoustic efficiency in a sung tone.
Fundamental	Lowest partial of a spectrum, the frequency of which normally corresponds to the pitch perceived.
Glottis	The space between the vocal folds.

Harmonic	A frequency that is an integer multiple of a given fundamental. Harmonics of a fundamental are equally spaced in frequency.
Head mix	Female music theater singing that is not pure head register production. The head register dominates, but a small amount of chest register is also present. It differs from classical singing in that the amount of chest voice used at any pitch level is more significant than in classical production.
Head register	A term used to describe singing produced primarily by the cricothyroid muscles of the throat. It derives its name from the vibrations felt in the head area while producing higher pitches. These vibrations are sympathetic and not produced in the head region. Although classical singing is dominated by the use of head voice, the use of chest voice is dominant in contemporary music theater repertoire.
High belt	Female chest register sung in the octave above middle C and, on some occasions, at higher pitches. In classical singing, the chest register is not used as predominantly in the middle C octave and above.
Hyoid bone	A horseshoe-shaped bone known as the "tongue bone." It is attached to muscles of the tongue and larynx.
Inharmonic	In music, inharmonicity is the degree to which the frequencies of overtones (also known as partials) depart from whole multiples of the fundamental frequency (harmonic series).
"Jukebox" musical	A musical that uses previously released popular songs as its musical score. Usually the songs have in common a connection with a particular popular musician or group.
Kilohertz	A kHz, or Kilohertz, is a measurement of frequency equal to 1,000 hertz. Kilohertz is a unit of measurement for alternating current, audio signals, and wireless signals.

Lamina propria   The tissue layers of the vocal folds below the outer epithelium.

Larynx   The cartilaginous box-shaped part of the respiratory tract located in the neck that includes the vocal folds. It is sometimes referred to as the "voice box." It is about the size of a walnut and attaches at the top to the hyoid bone. The larynx is capable of movement up and down, and this movement is the subject of a great deal of scientific investigation in belt singing. The scientific data generally show that in belting, the larynx assumes a high position, whereas in classical singing, it is in a lower position.

Lead sheet   A form of music notation that specifies the essential elements of a popular song: the melody, lyrics, and harmony. The melody is written in modern Western music notation, the lyric is written as text below the staff, and the harmony is specified with chord symbols above the staff.

Legit   The term used in music theater to describe male and female classical singing. It is a slang term shortened from the word *legitimate*. This term came into use to delineate between vaudeville and legitimate theater when legitimate theater first began. There are two types of legit singing: traditional and contemporary. The traditional legit sound has the qualities of classical singing, and the contemporary legit sound, while head voice dominant, is more speech-oriented. The speech component in contemporary legit singing results in a vocal sound that employs less classical resonance and has a brighter quality as opposed to the darker quality found in the traditional legit sound.

Light belt   Female chest register produced with very little pressure on the larynx or muscles of the throat. It is sometimes called "mixed" singing.

Loft voice   The highest (loftiest) register, usually referred to as falsetto voice.

Male belt   A controversial and understudied field. Some experts believe men belt, while others do not. The male belt voice differs from the female mix/belt voice. The belt component in men begins at the *passaggio* into the high range. At the high *passaggio*, the pharynx does not expand but stays in the speech position, and the vowels are not covered or modified. The low and middle ranges are not affected by the mix registration found in female music theater singers. Only the *passaggio* and above pitches are belted in the male music theater singer. The result is singing that is bright and speech-oriented.

Mariachi   A form of folk music from Mexico. The violin, vihuela, guitar, guitarron (bass guitar), and trumpet are the instruments most frequently used by the modern mariachi band.

Melodrama   Beginning in the eighteenth century, melodrama was a technique of combining spoken recitation with short pieces of accompanying music where music and spoken dialogue typically alternated, although the music was sometimes also used to accompany pantomime.

Minstrel show   An American entertainment consisting of comic skits, variety acts, dancing, and music, performed by White people in blackface or, especially after the Civil War, Black people in blackface. Minstrel shows lampooned Black people and began with brief burlesques and comic entr'actes in the early 1830s and emerged as a full-fledged form in the next decade.

Mix register   Used in music theater to describe a female singing sound that is a blend of head and chest register. The sound can be head register dominant with some chest or chest dominant with some head register. This mix blend can occur at any pitch level. Mix register is sometimes referred to as "blended" or "coordinated" register.

Modal voice   The vocal register used most frequently in speech and singing in most languages.

Overtone   Partial above the fundamental in a spectrum of sound.

Pantomime   An early music theater form that includes songs, slapstick comedy and dancing, and topical humor with a story loosely based on a well-known fairy tale. It developed partly from the sixteenth century commedia dell'arte tradition of Italy.

Partial   A partial is a higher tone produced at the same time as the lowest tone that helps to determine the overall quality of the sound. Overtones that are not whole-number multiples of the fundamental are called partials. In musical sounds, including singing, harmonic overtones strongly dominate. Partials, if present, lead to roughness and make correct intonation difficult to achieve. In singing, they are generally only found in damaged and dysfunctional voices.

Pharynx   The region above the larynx, below the velum, and posterior to the oral cavity (mouth). The pharynx is also described as a flexible tube that can stretch and constrict. Scientific studies generally show the pharynx in a stretched position during classical singing and a more closed position for music theater singing. These movements affect the movement of the larynx and the color of the sung sound. The stretched pharynx produces a "darker" color; the closed pharynx produces a "brighter" color.

Phonotrauma   Any abuse or misuse of the vocal folds, which leads to nodules, degenerative polyps, cysts, varices, papillomas, and other benign conditions.

Register   A unified group of tones that have the same texture or quality. In classical singing, the use of the head register predominates, whereas in music theater singing, especially for women, the use of chest register is favored.

Register balance   Describes the amount of chest and head register function in a sung tone. In music theater singing, this balance varies depending on the size of the voice and type of repertoire being sung.

Resonance   The peak occurring at certain frequencies in the vibration of sound.

Revue   A multiact popular theatrical entertainment that combines music, dance, and sketches. The revue has its roots in American popular entertainment and melodrama but grew into a substantial cultural presence of its own during its golden years from 1916 to 1932. Famous for their visual spectacle, revues frequently satirized contemporary figures, news, or literature.

Rhinosinusitis   An inflammation of the paranasal sinuses. It can be due to infection, allergy, or autoimmune issues. Most cases are due to a viral infection and resolve over the course of ten days. It is a common condition, with more than twenty-four million cases annually in the United States.

"Riff"   A brief, relaxed phrase repeated over changing melodies. It may serve as a refrain or melodic figure, often played by the rhythm section instruments or solo instruments that form the basis or accompaniment of a musical composition.

Singer's formant   A high spectrum peak occurring between about 2.3 and 3.5 kHz in voiced sounds in Western opera and concert singing. It is associated with the "ring" in a voice and with the voice's ability to project over the sound of a choir or orchestra.

Source   A theory that assumes the time-varying glottal
                          airflow to be the primary sound source.

"Space"   The most basic definition of space is that every note
                          written on the page can serve as a point of
                          departure. Space has several characteristics: the
                          pitch can be changed either up or down while
                          respecting the harmony; the note can become more
                          than one note (ornaments, repeated notes, etc.); the
                          note can be started earlier or later than written; and
                          the duration of notes can be changed.

Sprechstimme   A German term meaning "speech-voice." In music,
                          it is a cross between speaking and singing in which
                          the tone quality of speech is heightened.
                          Sprechstimme is frequently used in twentieth-
                          century music.

Subglottal   Air pressure in the airway immediately below the
pressure   level of the closed vocal folds.

Tessitura   Generally describes the most common pitch range
                          found in a given piece of music.

Through-sung   A term describing a musical with no spoken
                          dialogue.

Thyroarytenoid   A paired intrinsic laryngeal muscle that constitutes
muscle   the bulk of the vocal fold. It is also called the
                          vocalis muscle. The medial belly constitutes the
                          body of the vocal fold. It is the primary muscle used
                          in the production of the lower pitches in a singing
                          voice. It is also commonly referred to as the chest
                          voice muscle. Music theater singing is often
                          characterized by predominant use of the
                          thyroarytenoid or chest voice muscle. Music theater
                          singing often uses this muscle at higher pitches than
                          classical singing.

Thyroid cartilage   The largest laryngeal cartilage. It is open posteriorly
                          and is made up of two plates (thyroid laminae)
                          jointed anteriorly at the midline. In males, there is a
                          prominence superiorly known as the "Adam's

Apple" visible from the outside as a protrusion in the middle of the throat.

Typing

Music theater singers are cast in roles according to their physical and vocal "type." At auditions, the physical typing usually occurs first. Singers are eliminated before singing if they do not, in the director's opinion, meet the physical requirement of the role. Those fitting the physical requirements of the role are allowed to participate in the singing portion of the audition process.

Up-tempo

A term used in the music theater to describe a song that is characterized by a fast-moving tempo. Most music theater auditions require singers to audition with sixteen bars of an up-tempo selection and a ballad selection. The two choices provide contrast: one is slow, one is fast. The term up-tempo is used to describe all genres and styles found in music theater singing. In contrast, at classical singing auditions, it is assumed a variety of tempos will be included in the audition selections.

Variety show

A theatrical entertainment of successive separate performances of songs, dances, skits, and acrobatic feats.

Vaudeville

A theatrical genre of variety entertainment popular in the United States from the early 1880s until the early 1930s. Each performance was made up of a series of separate, unrelated acts grouped together on a common bill.

Vibrato

The periodic modulation of the frequency of phonation.

Vocal folds

The scientific term for a paired system of ligaments in the larynx that oscillate to produce sound. The vocal folds are sometimes referred to as vocal cords. The vocal folds consist of two wedge-shaped, multilayered bundles of muscles with ligamental edges covered by a mucous membrane. The vocal folds are a complex tensing and relaxing system; they can shorten, contract laterally, and vary both length and thickness during vibration, and part of them can even tense while the rest is relaxed.

Vocal ligament   Intermediate and deep layers of the lamina propria.

Voix mixte   The region of the singing voice in which sensations of "chest" and "head" registers are simultaneously experienced.

Zona di passaggio   The break between vocal registers.

APPENDIX

Conductor and Coach Interviews

TEN THINGS FOR ASPIRING MUSIC THEATER SINGERS TO KNOW

1. Musical theater is a dramatic art. This is the number one thing to keep in mind and strongly influences much of the following advice. Singers are often primarily musicians rather than actors, but Broadway singing must be guided more strongly by dramatic parameters than musical ones. Of course vocal technique and musicianship are very important, but they must be used as tools to serve the overarching dramatic needs. Choices of phrasing, vocal placement, tempo, strictness of rhythm, dynamics, and so on may be perfectly valid from a musical standpoint, but if they conflict with the character or the dramatic context then they are poor choices.

2. A broad spectrum of skills is necessary. Musicians become used to the notion that honing one specific skill as close to perfection as possible will lead to success. However, musical theater is a multiskill environment. The strongest singers in the world will not find success if they cannot also act or dance or both. Aspiring musical theater singers who already have strong vocal skills are better served putting more effort into learning to act and/or dance, rather than "perfecting" their singing voice. This is not to take away from the importance of maintaining a strong and versatile singing technique— just a reminder that better acting will im-

prove a singing audition much more effectively than marginally better or "more perfect" singing (assuming one already has professional-quality singing technique). I've seen many marginal singers who were strong actors win singing roles over far-better singers who did not have the acting skills.

3. Musical versatility is very helpful. Musical theater embraces many different musical and vocal styles. Not everyone can be equally good at them all. It's best to know what style you're most suited for and pursue those shows and roles. However, it's helpful to increase your knowledge and experience in singing in other styles, to maximize your versatility. Often actor/singers are required to "play against type" for comic or dramatic reasons. The more comfortable and versatile one is in as many different styles as possible, the more hirable one might be.

4. Musical literacy is very helpful, but not a prerequisite. Singers always help themselves by being more musically literate—that is, being able to read and sight-sing printed music, to follow and understand musical accompaniments, to recognize harmonic chord types and progressions, to comprehend standard Italian musical terminology, and so forth. These skills make learning new music much easier and faster, but they generally will not help you get work other than readings. I'm constantly working with actor/singers who are musically completely illiterate, other than being able to see that notes go up or down. These people continue to work steadily because they are very strong actors, and they sing well enough and can learn music by rote.

5. Singers must analyze, understand, and convey the text. Too many singers clearly do not understand the importance of the text. They're so consumed by the vocal and musical elements that they forget that the text is the predominant language of dramatic communication and not just sounds to vocalize on. The whole reason for a song in a musical is that a character must express a strong emotion or idea. Yes, the music and vocal melody participates crucially in that (and yes, there are times when writers intentionally eschew words or comprehensibility). But for the vast majority of songs, the words supply most of the content and must be the starting point for the singer's understanding of the song.

A singer must understand *what* is being said, *why* the character is choosing to say it, *who* the character is that is singing, and *how* the character feels about what he is saying. He must also take into account any potential things that are *not said* that may be part of his inner monologue. This is a dramatic analysis of the text. The singer should also analyze the craft of the lyric—the implicit rhythm of the words, the rhyme scheme (including less-obvious inner rhymes), how brittle or supple the words sound, etc.—and how that relates to the dramatic content.

Once a lyric is fully analyzed and understood in dramatic context, then the singer can pair it back with the music and often find deeper ways that the music supports or informs the text, leading to a richer and more deeply felt performance.

Finally, the singer must remember that the text must be intelligible to the listener if the writer's intention is to be fully realized. The act of singing can often obfuscate the clarity of words, especially in higher registers. Voice teachers often concentrate on vowel sounds since that's where the vocal resonance lies. But the singer must remember that consonants are more important for intelligibility and that they often must be overarticulated in order to be conveyed clearly. I particularly appreciate singers that "make a meal of the words." The listener cannot ride the journey of the song if he is struggling to make out the words.

6. Acting is about thoughts/emotions that lead to utterance. I can't teach acting in one paragraph of advice, but I can help illuminate a concept that most singers fail to realize: acting is not about what someone is feeling or doing while they are speaking/singing a text; rather, it is about the thoughts or feelings or actions that *lead* them to say/sing the text. A big part of the text analysis needs to be figuring out what those motivational keys are for the character and incorporating them into the performance of the song such that it appears that the character is responding to the inner impulse to utter words. More often than not, these words spring spontaneously from the character in the context of the situational moment, yet singers often deliver lyrics in a song that sound like the prewritten text that they are. Of course, the singer must know the prewritten text ahead of singing it, but most often the *character* should not, until the motivational thought triggers it. Being able to convincingly embody the cause-effect relationship of thoughts to words is what makes good acting in a song.

7. Be careful of back phrasing. These days, too many singers automatically back phrase anything with emotional content, often as a poor, lazy substitute for more specific acting. Back phrasing has its valid and powerful uses, often to convey a character's emotional difficulty with the text or a moment when the character must think of how to express a thought. The

musical tension that back phrasing creates can often heighten a climactic phrase in a song. However, the singer should bear in mind that back phrasing often bears diminishing returns—the more you back phrase in a song, the less effective it is. As a conductor, I hate it when I feel like I'm dragging a singer through a song, as if they're reluctant to sing it. A song ought to spring forth from a character because he feels an urgency to express a strong thought or emotion. The character should *drive* the song and compel the music to be formed and come along. It is not the music that should motivate the character to sing, but quite the other way around. There is great power to be harnessed by the singer singing the written rhythms on time and trusting the composer's choices.

8. Be intelligent about strictness of pitch and rhythm. This is somewhat related to back phrasing but a separate issue. Music uses a precise notational system of pitch and rhythm, but often too much precision is detrimental to a performance. Though we usually want the singer to sing "in tune," overly precise pitch precludes the dramatic use of inflection. If rhythms are too strictly adhered to, words may come over as too stilted. As in most music, a humanizing element needs to be applied, especially in musical theater singing, which is all about the human element. A good composer will strive to set lyrics in a rhythm that allows the words to retain a measure of their natural spoken rhythm, except when a specific dramatic or comic effect is being sought. The singer should take an intelligent approach to determining how strictly to interpret the musical writing. Much of the time, even-rhythms can be somewhat relaxed to sound more natural and communicative. However, like back phrasing, changing the rhythm should not be done mindlessly, and care should be taken not to change the composer's intent. Sometimes a more precise, stilted delivery is intended to heighten comedy, for instance. Or a specific rhythm might be an important motivic element to the song that should not be changed.

Most musical theater composers write/wrote in rather simple rhythms and expected singers to make the rhythms sound natural automatically. However, some more sophisticated composers (e.g., Leonard Bernstein, Stephen Sondheim, Stephen Schwartz, Jason Robert Brown) tend to write more exactly what they mean, even to the extent of writing out the back phrasing they want. Generally the more complicated the rhythm appears, the more strictly the composer intends for it to be adhered to, but the singer should always balance that intelligently with the dramatic needs of the character.

9. Be a team player with your accompanist. Whether you're singing with just piano accompaniment or being supported by a conductor with a pit or concert-orchestra, you should recognize your role in collaborating with your accompanist. Accompaniment does not happen magically, though many singers behave as such. A good conductor or pianist will breathe with the singer and anticipate phrasing choices in support of the singer. A good singer should reciprocate by helping the accompanist to anticipate what's coming. The best singers almost conduct the song themselves by use of their breath and body language.

10. Rules are meant to be broken! There are undoubtedly exceptions to every item in this list. As in any art, there is no such thing as perfection, and often better art is achieved by the judicious, conscious breaking of some rules. In musical theater singing (except perhaps in revue-style shows—there's your exception!), my number one rule ought to be the prevailing guide: Musical theater is a dramatic art. Any other rule can be broken if it is justified by dramatic circumstances. Your performance as a musical theater singer is enhanced by your singularity, your individualism, and your unique approach that differs from everyone else's. Discover how a song works for you, and own it. If it's dramatically compelling enough, it will be memorable and successful!

—Lawrence Goldberg

TOP TEN PIECES OF AUDITION ADVICE

1. If you've planned what to sing from your own repertoire, avoid changing songs at the last minute without good reason. It's natural to second-guess yourself when under pressure, but it's probably just your nerves talking. It's always better to avoid making important decisions when under the influence of adrenaline!

2. Trying to get through your entire song when asked for only sixteen bars shows that you don't know how to follow directions. However, since a bar is not a measure of time, requesting a certain number of bars of a

song is somewhat illogical. Remember that sixteen-bar auditions are essentially typecasting, to determine whether you will go on to the next step of the audition process. When cutting your song, keep in mind that the requested sixteen bars should equal about thirty-five to forty-five seconds that show you off at your best. If they're being literal about the number of bars you're permitted to sing, you'll have to be ready for that contingency with appropriate song cuts.

3. Know what you're singing about and to whom you're singing, as well as the meaning of every single word of the lyric. I recommend singing to one or more imaginary people and optionally including the actual people behind the table. When singing, don't worry too much about your hands. Motion is generated by emotion, and your physical movement should evolve from your subtext.

4. Think of the waiting room as a professional workspace, and try not to let others distract you from your impending audition. Make every effort to put aside any preconceived notions about what will happen since things constantly change in the audition room.

5. Avoid learning a new song for an audition unless required, and try not to audition with any song if you have doubts about your ability to sing it well. Worrying about hitting the last note may distract you throughout your performance. And don't bring any song into an audition room if it's not memorized and prepared. They have a tendency to thumb through your book.

6. Never snap or clap tempo to the accompanist. Give the tempo of your song by softly singing a bar or two. If the accompanist is unable to decipher markings on music or has multiple page turns, your audition may be sabotaged. The most important thing to indicate in music cuts is what you want the accompanist to play for your introduction. The more care you take in the presentation of your audition music, the more care the accompanist will give it.

7. Increase your repertoire to include more songs in more styles, so you are ready with appropriate audition material.

8. It's best to avoid "signature" songs that make us think of the original artists. If you sing "Don't Rain on My Parade," it will be difficult for the auditors not to think of Barbra Streisand or Lea Michele.

9. It's generally a good idea not to sing a song from the show you're auditioning for unless specifically requested. Why? There's no need to limit yourself to only that one role. And you don't want to appear locked

into a specific performance that might not match the director's vision of how that song should be done.

10. Remember that no matter what, there's always the next audition. In this business the only way to fail is to give up.

—Robert Marks (RobertMarks.com)

TIPS FOR CONDUCTORS

Rhythm and Tempo

Read the chapter on "Rhythm and Tempo" in Richard Boleslavsky's *Acting: the First Six Lessons* (http://www.amazon.com/Acting-First-Lessons-Richard-Boleslavsky/dp/1626549974/ref=sr_1_1?s=books&ie=UTF8&qid=1372030157&sr=1-1&keywords=boleslavsky).

Metronome markings should be thought of as approximations. Don't use tempo as an absolute to torment singers.

I have heard many, many performances in which the pulse essentially stayed at about eighty to ninety beats to the minute. I call this the "default tempo." Strive for variety in tempo, if only to keep your audience awake.

Always communicate with the choreographer. You may like a tempo, but if the dancers can't do it expressively at that speed, your work is worthless.

Conducting

Don't lean back and conduct at your singers; lean forward with inclusive, embracing gestures, if possible.

Large, generous gestures communicate a better line and facilitate better breathing. Use the words to help them to sing rhythmically. Too much subdivision of the beat is unclear and confusing.

Don't clap the rhythm! It makes people tense, and if you do something audible at the same time you want someone else to do it, it's too late. That's what upbeats and "gestures of syncopation" are for.

It's perfectly good to mouth the words if you must to keep the singers together, but don't sing, except to demonstrate. You can't hear them if you sing.

Sir Henry Wood, English conductor and a very efficient rehearser, said: "The conductor must not be afraid of the art of gesture." Find a way to show them what you want; don't take time telling them, unless you really have to.

Working with Singers

Many singers read music less well than instrumentalists; some read not at all. Never feel you have the right to embarrass or punish them. Your only valid choice is patience and respect for their ability to make a beautiful and expressive sound.

This may horrify some purists, but if a choral number ends with a big, loud chord, it's often fun to let the chorus "fake" the last chord—to sing the note they would prefer to sing, as long as it's "in the chord." It's usually in their best range, though you may have to adjust the balance sometimes.

—Mort Stein

INDEX

ABOUT THE AUTHOR AND CONTRIBUTORS

In 2006, **Karen Hall** graduated from Teachers College, Columbia University, with a doctor of education degree. She also holds a bachelor and master of music degree in vocal performance from the University of Houston. Additional study in operetta was completed at the Mozarteum Summer Academy in Salzburg, Austria. The Contemporary Commercial Music (CCM) Vocal Pedagogy Institute sponsored by Shenandoah University has also certified her at Levels I, II, and III.

An active member of the National Association of Teachers of Singing (NATS), in 2012 she was appointed one of six associate editors for the *Journal of Singing*; in 1995 was chosen to be a NATS intern; and has served on the NATS board of directors, Boston chapter, and on the Board of the New York Singing Teachers Association (NYSTA). While working toward her doctoral degree, she was invited to join Kappa Delta Pi, an honor society in education. A frequent master class clinician and adjudicator, Karen has been invited to present master classes at the Longy School of Music, Emory and Henry College, and East Carolina University and has adjudicated at numerous district and regional NATS events and voice competitions.

A versatile performer, Karen has performed in opera, operetta, concert, oratorio, recital, chamber music, and music theater throughout the United States. She is a five-time Metropolitan Opera Regional Finalist and has won awards from the Texas Federation of Music Clubs, the Vocal

Arts Foundation in San Francisco, and the Eleanor Anderson Lieber Awards, sponsored by Portland Opera.

She has four recordings to her credit: *The Frogs* and *Sweeney Todd* both by Stephen Sondheim; *American Songs in Recital*, a solo CD of American art songs and music theater selections; and the Pulitzer prize–winning recording *On the Transmigration of Souls* by John Adams, recorded with the New York Philharmonic Orchestra.

Karen resides in Santa Fe, New Mexico; serves as the series editor for So You Want to Sing: A Guide for Professionals, a series of vocal pedagogy books being produced in partnership with Rowman & Littlefield and the National Association of Teachers of Singing; and teaches in her private studio, Songwerks. Previously, Karen has been a faculty member at the Crane School of Music/SUNY Potsdam, the Boston Conservatory, the Berklee School of Music in Boston, New York University, and East Carolina University. During the summer of 2010, Karen was a visiting professor at Mahidol University in Bangkok, Thailand.

Karen's research and subsequent teaching guide concerning music theater vocal pedagogy has been recognized by the College Music Society, the National Association of Teachers of Singing, the Voice Symposium, and the Texoma NATS Artist Series in the form of invitations to present poster presentations and lectures. In 2011, the Fulbright Organization approved Karen's application to become a Fulbright specialist. As a Fulbright specialist, she will travel to foreign universities to share her research and teaching specialty—contemporary vocal pedagogy.

Contributor **Scott McCoy**, DMA, professor of voice and pedagogy at The Ohio State University, is the director of the Helen Swank Voice Teaching and Research Lab. He has been professor of voice and pedagogy, director of the Presser Music Center Voice Laboratory, and the director of Graduate Studies at Westminster Choir College of Rider University. His multimedia voice science and pedagogy textbook, *Your Voice, An Inside View*, is used extensively by colleges and universities throughout the United States and abroad. He is immediate past president and director of the National Intern Program of the National Association of Teachers of Singing (NATS) and associate director of the *Journal of Singing* for voice pedagogy and has also served NATS as vice president for workshops, program chair for the 2006 and 2008 national conferences, chair of the Voice Science Advisory Committee, and master teacher for the National

Intern Program. Deeply committed to teacher education, McCoy is a founding faculty member in the NYSTA Professional Development Program, teaching classes in voice anatomy and physiology and acoustics and voice analysis. He is a member of the distinguished American Academy of Teachers of Singing.

Contributor **Wendy DeLeo LeBorgne**, PhD, CCC-SLP, is the director of the Blaine Block Institute for Voice Analysis and Rehabilitation (Dayton, Ohio) and the Professional Voice Center of Greater Cincinnati (Cincinnati, Ohio). She holds a BFA in musical theater from Shenandoah Conservatory (Winchester, Virginia) and both her masters and doctoral degrees from the University of Cincinnati in communication sciences and disorders with a specialty in voice disorders. Her research has focused primarily on the area of the professional singing voice (specifically the Broadway belt voice).